Into the Heart
Of Africa

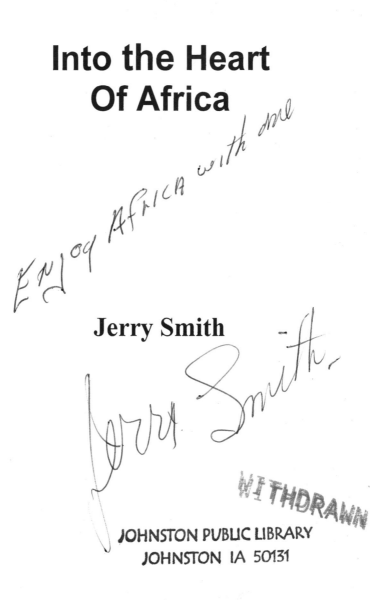

Enjoy Africa with one

Jerry Smith

Copyright © 2000
Jerry Smith

Library of Congress Control Number: 00-90663

ISBN: 978-0-9701930-0-1

Seventh Printing 2010

For color pictures go to www.theheartofafrica.com

Additional copies of this book are available by mail from
Jerry Smith
102 West 5th Street
Hedrick, IA 52563
641-653-4436

Printed in the United States by
Morris Publishing
3212 East Highway 30
Kearney, NE 68847
1-800-650-7888

For My Family

Front Cover - The photo of baobab trees taken above the Great Riff Valley echoes the environment where the great beasts live. These massive trees provide a haven for many creatures that fly or climb and may hold the spirits of their countless ancestors.

ACKNOWLEDGEMENTS

Without the love, encouragement and support of my family, my three-month trek Into the Heart of Africa would not have been possible. I also owe a debt of gratitude to family members and friends for their advice and technical assistance in preparing my adventure for publication.

Photo of The Author with his wife, Josefina, and their daughter, Belinda. [Photo by Sherm Cooper]

TABLE OF CONTENTS

INTRODUCTION

In my youth I retained but one textbook. It was J. Russell Smith's Human Geography. The author explained that geography is the relationship between the earth and the life that lives upon it. The contents of this textbook fueled my desire to see and feel those far-away places with the strange sounding names.

In the formative years of my youth, my brother Mike and I spent many afternoons searching for the unusual in the rolling tree-covered hills and along the rocky streambeds of VanBuran County, Iowa.

By the time I was eighteen I had my first motorcycle, and I began to travel and explore. These trips invariably turned into adventures, as I would be overwhelmed with curiosity wondering where an old road would lead or where a narrow canyon trail would end. My quest for adventure continued into adulthood but frequently included my courageous wife Jo.

On one such adventure Jo and I were exploring the back roads of El Salvador in Central America. We had left the highway and were descending a long, sandy road. At the bottom of a hill we turned left crossing a fifteen-foot-wide shallow stream. As we ascended the far bank, five or six gunmen bolted from behind the trees pointing their guns toward our heads. We came to an abrupt stop.

Until that moment I had never known what an alert thinker and brave woman my Mexican wife is. As we came to a stop, she told me, "Jerry, just look down and let me handle it. A Latin will not shoot a woman."

Jo dismounted, walked over and stood between the gunmen and me. It may have been that they were married men and didn't want a confrontation with another woman. Whatever the reason, they backed off. In a few minutes the leader waved his six-shooter and pointed it toward the way we came in. Jo remounted the cycle telling me, "Just turn the thing around and leave. They won't shoot us in the back." We left without a comment or a second look.

The following year I was formulating plans to cycle the perimeter of the African continent on my same BMW. During this period I received an invitation from Bill Record of Manchester, New York, to join him and a group of men to cross Africa diagonally using on/off road motorcycles. Even though our daughter Belinda was but one-year-old, Jo told me, "You must go. This will be the greatest trip of them all." Her blessing was imperative for an adventure of this magnitude.

Preparations began immediately. I became totally focused on setting my personal and business affairs in order and on studying maps of the thirteen African countries and the physical extremes of Africa that we would pass through. These physical extremes include North Africa's Atlas Mountains and the Sahara, the world's largest desert. Beyond the desert stretches the Sahel, a thousand-mile-wide belt of sugar sand, thorn-tree forest and grasslands. Then come vast rolling hill country, river crossings and the broad jungles of Equatorial Africa to be followed by the immense East African savanna, the mountain ranges and more of the enormous savanna where herds of those famous wild animals roam. Our trek would lead on east and south beyond the equator until the stinging hot water of the Indian Ocean's coral reef was reached at the extreme southern tip of Kenya just 1 degree 30" north of the island of Zanzibar.

Bill Record, who planned and was the strategist for our journey, purchased the motorcycles that proved 100 percent dependable. Fuel mileage was good; suspension and handling were acceptable. All were to be delivered in a campground south of Malaga, Spain.

As preplanned, all eleven riders arrived at the JFK International Airport in New York and met in a room provided by KLM Airlines. Within the brief time of our meeting and boarding the Boeing 747, it became evident that two of our group were apprehensive at this risky undertaking. Everyone else, like thoroughbreds led to the starting gates of the Kentucky Derby, was hyped ready to go.

Three-and-a-half days after leaving New York and before sunrise, we rode our bikes into the ship that would ferry us across the Strait of Gibraltar. After securing my bike, I hurried up the steel stairway into the still, near-darkness. It was a clear, cool morning with a soft chilly breeze blowing in from the Atlantic.

Looking back east, I could see the Rock of Gibraltar -- dark, nearly black, but the outline over its massive perimeter was the yellowish-blue glow from the rising sun. That morning, while still in Algeciras, Spain's harbor, the sun rose over Europe. In the evening it set over Africa.

The seamen cast off the lines; a fine vibration ran through the ship. We were moving at last. As our big vessel passed the breakers, she began a slight rolling motion. Within the hour sunlight was shining on the low mountain of Mt. Hacho, Africa. We have all felt the excitement of the final hour after weeks of preparations. For me, this was the ultimate.

Now come ride with me, and together we'll share what was one of the greatest motorcycle adventures of all time.

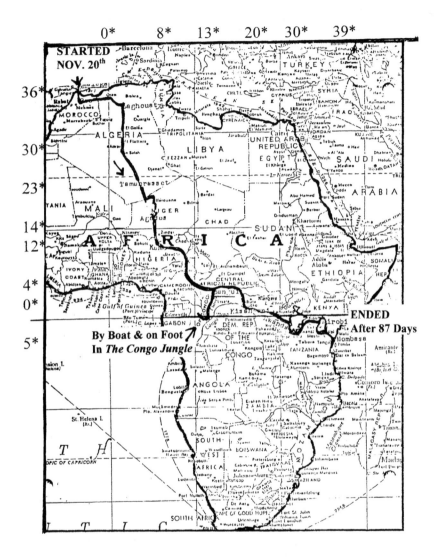

I

GHETTO OF THIEVES
36 Degrees North – 5 Degrees West

Entering into the heart of Africa was just minutes away as I left the handrails of the main deck of our good ship that had ferried us from Algeciras, Spain, across the Straight of Gibraltar into the harbor of Ceuta. Finding the stairwell, I hurried down the steel steps letting my left hand slide against the banister until reaching the ship's next lower level.

This lower level was dimly lit by a few rows of small incandescent bulbs. Finding my bike was not difficult. This bike would be my constant companion for the next three months. I would eat with it, sleep with it and ride it while exploring the interior of the Dark Continent. My motorcycle was tied to the forward starboard side with a nylon line looped around the handlebars and drawn tight against the hard board slats made for securing cargo.

I jerked the loose end of the holding line, then threw my right leg over the saddle. It was just minutes to wait until the ship's big doors opened wide. For the first time, from the saddle of my bike, I saw a sampling of the blue skies over Africa.

I've rolled by bikes to the starting line of race tracks hundreds of times. But never had I experienced the excitement and expectation as that felt rolling near the exit ramp in anticipation of charging out into the world's largest playground. This playground is so vast; it takes months to cross.

Before the doors were latched into their open position I had clicked my tranny into first gear and had accelerated down the ship's ramp onto the pastel gray concrete piers of Ceuta's sunny harbor.

Ceuta, owned by the Spanish, is a small, picturesque, strategic enclave across from Gibraltar. This city wasn't planned to be a stopping point on our diagonal three-month trip crossing the African continent. But, because of upcoming problems at the Ceuta/Morocco border, we were detained within Ceuta for a few days.

It was just an hour's ride out to the frontier where the only legal overland crossing point out of this municipality was located. The border crossing was to the east and located adjacent to Morocco where the hills from the interior reach the Mediterranean.

On arrival at the checkpoint, we stopped at the gates and went inside the narrow, one–story immigration building. The officer in charge was seated behind a mahogany colored, wooden desk with nothing on its top but the forms he was using.

He was a clean-shaven fellow in his late thirties, wearing a well-pressed tan uniform. Between his army officer's hat and his necktied collar, was the face of a no nonsense, square-jawed, Dick Tracy. It was quite evident this officer in charge was not the type of person to sit around reading the local newspaper while drinking coffee and participating in small talk.

Rather, after returning our papers, he informed us that we would not be permitted to pass without an explanation. Because of his repugnant attitude, we refrained from questioning his authority or military clout. During the hours and days following, we would try crossing again and again, but he was always on duty and inflexible.

Waiting for an attitude change and remembering the 1898 Spanish American War, I pondered his obstinacy. Was he bitter at something Teddy Roosevelt possibly uttered inadvertently while he and the "Rough Riders" were charging up San Juan Hill?

Or did he believe some unfounded rumors regarding who blew up their flagship, *The Spanish Main*, in the Havana harbor. Another thought, he was having a nicotine withdrawal headache, blaming us Americans for a shortage of Havana Cigars.

2

Whatever his unfounded excuse, it was left to rest while we departed from the frontier to enjoy the charms of historic Ceuta and to secure a remote camping site.

Finding a place to camp was soon solved when we made an acquaintance with a sharply dressed Sergeant Major in Spain's army. He was riding a white R26BMW motorcycle, of which he was justly proud and enjoying thoroughly. Riding together with the sergeant, he took us to a pleasant, old Spanish restaurant, a soccer game and on a winding tour through the narrow mountain streets. We finished our ride at the summit of Mt. Hacho. We camped in a military park on top of this mountain, Africa's version of Gibraltar.

The park was well maintained, grassy throughout with small but broadly branched shade trees. From this vantage point, we could see two continents as well as where the waters of the Atlantic and Mediterranean converge. To reach the park we used a narrow, one way, six–mile, winding road. It was a real blast to play on, especially exciting at night on the last run.

One of our riders, Sherm Cooper, from Trenton, New Jersey, was in the lead and doing a beautiful job to a point. At the last switchback before the summit, he overshot the turn by a country mile. His XL250 Honda launched off the banked switchback turn like Evel Kenevil's last jump in the Astrodome. The biker's trajectory ended within the limbs of a broad-branched shade tree a good ten or twelve feet above the ground. The cycle did quite well for itself only needing a long rope and a couple of parts to be ready to go again.

As for Sherm Cooper, he didn't fare so well. Once he was out of the saddle, he was out of control. He tried a barrel–roll and only got it partially completed. Then instead of a controlled glide on a grassy knoll, he did a head and shoulder upside–down crash into General Franco's prize chainlink fence.

Now this wasn't just any run-of-the-mill prize fence of General Franco. It was the fence that kept the riffraff and gringos from crashing down on Spain's huge sixteen inch Big Bertha shore batteries. Hitting this fence not

3

only shook the fence, but apparently shook up two machine gun toting army guards who weren't in any mood to pitch in and help. At least the people of Spain could sleep because the shore gun operators couldn't.

As for Sherm's injuries, much of the time during the next three months he wore an away–from–home, homemade neck brace cut from an inch–thick rubber bumper pad.

With the morning's fresh sun and a day to play, I had plenty of time to find the good, the bad and the ugly. This was not my intention. But I did have all the ingredients for success. I had a full tank of gas, a bike that loved to be ridden and a wanderlust that craved adventure.

After a good breakfast I started south, crossing by bridge the Portuguese Walls Moat, part of a huge fortification built entirely across the isthmus centuries ago. The fortification was constructed from light brown stone. The parapet relied on its broad width and the depth of the moat with nearly vertical walls, to become virtually unpenetratable.

Leaving the isthmus, I kept to the right at each road juncture until I was riding the outer perimeter.

Riding the outer perimeter of Ceuta, Spain, which has a common border with scorned Morocco, would turn out to be not only a long but also an exciting adventure. First of all, I ran face to face into a squad of Spanish soldiers who were marching in a broad formation. Having no place else to go on the narrow road, I turned my XL250 up a side street, not knowing they had the same direction in mind. Now with them coming behind me, I turned left again, this time into a lady's driveway where she was hanging clothes to dry. She didn't scream, the troops didn't shoot and no husband came running out. While the soldiers were approaching with their rhythmic four-count beat, I sat on my idling motorcycle listening and watching Spain's finest.

I felt very out of place and just as soon as this dressy, infantry outfit passed, I was on my way to see

4

what the Moors and then the Spaniards had done to this outcropping of Africa's Northwest corner.

Going west and south the road wound along the rocky Atlantic coast reaching the Moroccan frontier in a mountainous region. There I observed a few army lookouts using binoculars, watching something on the far side of the canyon. These were the only people I had seen since leaving the town area. No one was using the coastal border road but me.

Turning east still on this perimeter road, off to the left I saw a few Muslims with a small flock of sheep pasturing extremely beautiful rolling timberland. The eastward road after leaving the Atlantic coast roughly paralleled the Moroccan border.

Not riding more than twenty or twenty–five miles an hour I started to hear projectiles whistling overhead. A short distance away there was a jeep sitting crossways in the road. I felt like a sitting duck in a shooting gallery. Bringing my bike nearer to the jeep, I piled off, ran into a field and jumped into an old grassy foxhole with four dogface boys of Franco's army of the outback.

It certainly didn't seem like a good idea to surprise these guys with guns. When I made my feet- first jump wearing a blue, duckbilled, Arthur Fulmer motorcycle helmet, they must have thought the army doesn't pay enough.

The four GI's in full uniform and helmets, seemed relaxed and not tense with a white-knuckled grip on their weapons. No doubt this wasn't the only foxhole with combatants. The four militants simply sat there as if it were time for the afternoon cocoa, while I was rising up trying to see what was happening. I couldn't hear any explosions or see any smoke in either direction, just the overhead shriek of projectiles. Among all the trees in the area, if bullets were flying I could have heard the directional zipping of the slugs through the leaves. Everything seemed so peaceful except for the undeviating, constant shrieking above.

In a few minutes the shelling, or whatever it was, stopped. I climbed out, going to my bike without making

5

eye contact with anyone. Starting my bike's engine, I let it idle for a while, hesitating long enough to get a feel of the local situation. By then it seemed halfway safe to continue east. However, it was strange that no one was up there in those beautiful, rolling, mountainous hills except a few soldiers and myself on this sunny November afternoon in 1974.

I accelerated away slowly, still on this narrow, twisting, turning road that followed a high ridge inland. As I rode on, I saw one of the giant silo–shaped lookout towers that face the Moroccan border. There were five of these large towers that could be seen from below in the flatlands near the city. I approached this yellow sandstone lookout station, which must have been eight or ten stories high, with castellated battlements.

Unable to see any soldiers but not making any foolish moves, I took my camera and held it high above my head. From above the castellated battlements an arm shot straight up holding a big military rifle. We had no problems whatsoever communicating. I put my camera down and he lowered his rifle.

Keeping the frontier to my right, the narrow road bent left around a rather large trash–cluttered hill, which was unusual in clean Spain. At the base of this ascent was a 'T' road. I could either continue and return to the safety of the city or turn right into an area that was rummaged by the disadvantaged minority.

Turning right, the track veered right and left to miss washouts in the dry, hard clay. Useless cans, paper and refuse of the poorest of the poor were all over until I turned left at the summit of the knoll and rode directly into a community of low, small shacks made of tin from old signs, junk wood, and anything else to make a shelter. It was evident these were not family dwellings of the poorest. Rather they were shelters built by the lowest class of criminal element who no doubt obtained the building materials by scavenging or stealing.

In the recent past, some outfit had come through their street with a large-nozzle sprayer, painting each and every little dwelling with a thick blue paint. That probably took care of the lice on the outside. A few of the shanties with windows had some of the blue paint scraped enough to let in a little light.

An indication of things to come was exemplified by the conduct of the first person I saw. A hard-faced, half-dressed guy came running from between the shanties as hard as he could, trying to grab onto my bike. I sped up a bit and he missed. But more young men joined the chase. I had never been in a completely lawless ghetto where the occupants were mean tempered tough thugs. It was evident that the strongest of the mob rules. There couldn't have been sanctuary in one's home, and no woman could have retained her chastity in such a savage environment. At the "T" intersection I made my choice. Now it was up to me to see if I could live with this witless decision.

It was too late to turn back as a mob had formed. The problem was not outrunning the horde. The problem was that all streets sooner or later came to an end, and this one ended too soon. There were no side streets, and no way back around in this hilltop community.

There was a flat area where the street ended, then a steep descent to a leveled off lower plane with a high wire fence and an open gate. Two men were working at the crest when I started over, one an older fellow, one younger. I pointed to the open gate at the bottom of the hill. The older fellow shook his head, the younger nodded. Knowing the older man was giving good advice, I had no other choice but to descend the hill and ride on through the gate with the mob I had just outrun back at the top of the hill.

Seeing three Berber women standing at the gate gave me no indication of what I was really seeing. It only looked to me like three large gals in their natural, gray, wool robes. On closer inspection I observed that within each garment the wearer was enjoying the closeness of her uniformed boyfriend.

Turning left toward the Mediterranean along a smooth, sandy road, I felt tremendous relief after being pursued just minutes before. Now I was relaxing and calculating where I was in relationship to returning to the city of Ceuta.

To my right was pastureland with small trees. To my left was a tall fence with barbed wire entanglement. Seeing the barbed wire entanglement to my left meant I had crossed into Morocco. That is why the older man shook his head when I was descending toward the gate. My stomach cramped with anxiety as I realized that if I ran into a Moroccan patrol or tried crossing back without papers, they would put me in detention and throw away the beans.

I had no alternative but to turn back. I slowed to low gear, made a U-turn, knowing I would have to blow that gate, hit the hill at full throttle and face the mob head on.

Approaching the gate, this time in my way were three soldiers standing spread–eagle with their rifles held crosswise and three robed women over by the fence. I realized a number of things. First, those soldiers were there all the time inside the garments enjoying the intimacy of their suitors. Secondly, I had to confuse them. No way would I stop and take a chance of being thrown into Moroccan detention.

There were some points in my favor. Other than disturbing their afternoon recreation, I had not given them reason to be unhappy with me. There were no officers in the area for them to answer to. Also, I recognized those old Moroccan army issue World War I type, slow-loading, bolt action guns weren't nearly as frightening as burp guns would have been. I was thinking that If I could hit the gate at speed, I'd be up and over that hill in four or five seconds. I really didn't think they would shoot me. It was worth the gamble.

I approached the soldiers, who had blocked the road but not the gate. I swung wide to the left to give me a good angle at the opening while running at a pretty good speed in third gear. To confuse them, I stood up on the footpegs waving my left arm back and forth, screaming at the top of my lungs, "No, No, No."

8

Just as I neared the gate opening, I dropped to the saddle, hit second gear at full throttle, shot through the gate while lying flat on the gas tank "S'ing" it up and over the hill. And, as I thought, they had no intention of shooting, or if they did they never got a round shoved into the chamber and a bead on me in time. I certainly hoped it was the former.

Still ahead I needed to get past the mob that had just chased me down the same and only street of escape a few minutes before.

I observed a horde of twenty–five to thirty young thieves with no direction or previous thought but to chase en masse, each having the lust to grab and steal.

Riding toward the street thugs, keeping them close, I started turning in a circle to the right going just fast enough to keep the bandits excited thinking they were about to catch me. An unexpected surprise was quickly averted when the young scoundrel, who earlier had motioned me down the hill, wanted in on the spoils after the bandits had subdued me. He came across from up the hill. All I had to do was dodge left to make him miss, then right again to keep off the hillside. Never looking back at my hopeful street exit to prevent telegraphing my intentions, I kept leading them away within the very limited area near the top of the ridge.

It was a race for my life. I was turning right and shifting gears at full throttle simultaneously. My tires were over the crest of the hill causing the rear tire to slip and spin wildly on the dry, loose off-camber surface.

From my right side view I could see a group of men bent over pumping their arms, running frantically, straining to the limit to catch me. My engine revved quickly forcing me to power shift again while just over the hill's edge. Again the rear tire lost traction and spun off to the left. I reduced throttle to regain traction putting me up and over the crest of the hill toward the roadway out.

Then, getting near the drop–off edge, the mob started to cut across. I made a hard right at full throttle, attempting to finish my full circle by outflanking them on the left. By the time these lawless bandits at the back

9

could turn around, I was shifting gears at full throttle. It became a race, I finishing my diversionary circle and they racing back to cut me off before I reached the street to go out.

I swung wide to gain more speed and to give me more distance causing them to entirely cross the street. With a good fifteen feet to spare, I was past them and on my way out. On to the end of their only passage, I turned right, down the hill of trash. Darkness was setting in.

When I needed to move fast, it was better I was alone. The consequence of ill fate or hesitation would have had no reprieve. Reaching the foot of the hill, riding slowly, I thanked my Savior and my ability to recognize those turkeys' shortcomings of chasing as a mob.

There is a slogan: "To finish second is to be the first loser." If I had finished second in that convict colony, it could have been my final event. From the morning until evening darkness, I spent the entire day with no food or water, dodging, running; and what did I find in Ceuta's outback? The good, the bad and the ugly.

II

SMUGGLER
36 Degrees North – 5 Degrees West

One day at the frontier's checkpoint I spent hours waiting and watching. I had parked my bike outside the crossing area and brought my all-weather jacket to sit on while much of the time leaning with one elbow on my helmet. My vantage point was from the top of an outside retaining wall on the grass where I could lean back comfortably against the chain link fence. Rather than watching the blue-green waters of the Mediterranean on this sunny, breezeless day, I dedicated my time to watching the border guards practice their exercise of daily frustration. From this panorama, I witnessed repeated dramas of life unfold. From where I sat watching, an author such as Hemingway could have gathered enough material for a novel.

Moroccan women crossing back into their country were obviously carrying more contraband under their coarsely woven, gray robes than Harpo Marx carried inside his coat on a Vaudeville stage. The Spanish guards in their military hats and dark tan uniforms would kick, hit, shove and probe them with cane–length clubs but to no avail. Even with physical and verbal abuse, stumbling at times from the blows, these individuals kept maintaining their way past the checkpoint without expression or noticeable complaint.

Then there was Mr. Slick. To see this master of the shell game do his smuggling act was pure entertainment. First, when the bus stopped, he stepped down from the back door of the bus keeping one hand inside, as if he were just getting some fresh air. While the inspectors examined luggage being carried out from the front door of the bus, as no one was looking, he placed a small suitcase

11

on the ground and pushed it out of sight behind the foldout step with his foot. Now, the next part of his innocent act was going through the line and out the front door where the other passengers were holding their cases after examination. When all persons and known luggage were examined, an inspector went through looking under seats and overhead racks making sure all was accounted for.

When the inspector came out, the passengers began entering the bus using both doors. Mr. Slick, staying next to the bus as the line was boarding, merely bent over picked up his case, thus entering Ceuta with, no doubt, a quantity of Moroccan hashish.

A middle-aged man, slow and inconspicuous, was standing near the Mediterranean tidal wall under a small–leafed tree next to the back of the inspector's station. His face was iron gray, leathery, with cheekbones protruding high and a photographic facial profile. How long he had been there, I don't know, but I had been watching him for ten minutes or so.

A convenient diversionary distraction occurred and apparently everyone looked but me. I knew what the old boy was waiting for. When it happened, he jumped over the tidal wall onto the beach and vanished. I watched the wall to the west where the tidal wall turned north. I could see the man of the desert slowly walking. Where the sandbar came high along the wall, he was able to climb up and over, disappearing again, this time into the city.

Trying to cross from the Spanish province of Ceuta into Morocco lasted three days as well as some night attempts. The same crew was on duty twenty–four hours a day, as are some of our stateside fire departments. We just had to keep trying until a different squad of inspectors was on duty, which would be more favorable to our crossing out of their country.

We never knew why the officer in charge would not let us pass through immigration. It may have been the hijacked airliner at the airport in Tunnis at that time.

Possibly he was not acquainted with our motorcycles' abilities to travel; or more probably, he came from a large family, and when the dish of consideration was passed, his portion was already depleted. On the fourth day another group was on duty, and with just the routine paperwork, we were riding through Morocco.

Algerian mounted police patrol the intersection where our trek turned south.

III

COLD IN THE HIGH PLATEAUS
33 DEGREES NORTH - 4 DEGREES EAST

The road from Oran, Algeria, continued to the east. At this juncture we were leaving the sanctuary of city and farms and beginning the distant trek toward the Sahara Desert. Heading south was a turning point to remember.

Sitting at the "T" intersection were two BMW motorcycle mounted police. Thinking it would be interesting to visit with them, I pulled over and stopped. There were not enough vehicles on the road to warrant traffic control. However, they told me the president of Algeria was coming by, so these English-speaking police were there at that station to help with security.

Within a few minutes all of us were shocked by the speeding vehicles and the screaming sirens from the president's caravan. There were four black limousine-type vehicles and two ambulances traveling at a hundred miles per hour or more and staying close to each other even at such a high rate of speed. If our presidents used that method of conveyance, there would have been no need to limit their terms in office.

Crossing the high Atlas and Sahara Atlas Mountains was unusually interesting with their narrow, twisting roads passing over and around the old worn ranges and down through eroded gorges. Stopping in towns while still in the highlands, we were greeted by local kids who flocked around us by the dozens. Dark eyed, black hair and handsome, these young Berbers were fun to be around. They were totally excited seeing us and our motorcycles.

Not only were the highlands extremely old but also in some areas devoid of plant life. There was an area for a hundred miles or so where I occasionally saw turtle doves,

14

the gray cooing lovebirds.   It reminded me of my homeland.

We refueled our bikes and support truck in Laghouat still in the Atlas high plateau. It was there that I met and entered into a long conversation with an American and his wife who were there visiting for a day or so. He worked for the American Consulate in Algiers and while a student in the Foreign Service was a schoolmate of Jim Hargrove, who did his last work in Managua, Nicaragua, as the American Consulate.   This was the person who caused my wife much grief while I was awaiting trial during my detention in the Granada, Nicaragua, prison.

I had hit a seventy-two year old canefield worker by the name of Juan Rios. He had inadvertently walked in front of my BMW motorcycle on the highway south of Granada.   He was critically injured.   I was taken to detention in the Granada prison where I faced vehicular homicide if Sr. Rios died.

The following day my wife Jo, alone, took buses to the American Consulate in the capital city of Managua. It was there that the Consulate, Mr. Hargrove, told my wife, "We'll make sure your husband is treated fairly. If a 'Nic' is hanged with a new rope, we'll make sure your husband gets a new rope." Later, I was found not guilty of causing injury from a highway accident.

The Nicaraguan people with whom my wife came in contact treated her respectfully and with concern.   Jim Hargrove's office lady particularly befriended my wife Jo. And because of the friendship, this lady, whom I never met, worked for three days with Nicaragua immigration seeking permission for my wife and me to leave their country. With only twenty minutes remaining before their office would close for Christmas vacation, she secured our passage out.

My treatment in detention was without any transgressions.   The court, without prejudice, heard all the evidence and found me not guilty of causing injury to Sr. Rios.

That night during Christmas of 1972, an earthquake destroyed Managua along with nineteen thousand persons either killed or unaccounted for, including the dear lady who gained our passage. The hotel we would have returned to that night had no survivors. Jim Hargrove, by his own hand, gave up his life a day or two later. Even with the setting sun, the shadow of memory ceaselessly returns.

Because of my extended conversation with the American couple, I got a late start out of Laghouat. I headed south by myself, riding flat out trying to catch up before the next gas stop, which would be from the support truck. I didn't make it. Realizing too late that I was in a dilemma, I slowed down to conserve fuel.

In this barren no man's land, it started getting dark about the time my main tank supply ran out, and I had to switch to reserve. After going on reserve, I again slowed even more, hoping to travel twenty or more miles before the engine stopped completely. Because of the pleasant temperature during the day, I had put my Belstaff riding suit in the truck. That was the last time I went without my gear accompanying me at all times. That didn't help then, as with the setting sun, so went the heat. And I became very cold.

Riding slowly into the evening's darkness, my engine didn't sputter. It just stopped. I was already cold and the temperature was dropping. I stepped off my bike in this high desert where the sand is coarse and drifts but a little.

Using my binoculars, I was looking around the horizon trying to see if there was anything that could help. Off to the east in the last glow of evening, I could see two or three large, low, dark tents. There was a small ravine or large dry wash between us. I was thinking of the pros and cons of going there. Could I climb the sand side of this ravine? What would the nomadic tribesmen do or think of my coming out by myself in the desert night?

The unknown caused me to remain where I was. The cold was becoming bitter. I needed to do something.

There was a dried desert bush. I pulled it up and crumbled the bush. Then I placed a lighted match on the small pile I had made. In a flash it was gone. It provided no heat, just a flash of light. The Arabs could have seen it from the other side of the ravine, which gave me an uncomfortable feeling. Knowing the harshness of desert life, I knew that an aggressive Arab with a silent swing of a sword could obtain a set of my clothes, my photogray glasses and a pair of shoes, leaving a sad widow back home.

I considered taking a tool from my bike's tool bag and digging a hole in the sand to see if I could survive the night in a sandpit. Possibly the sand had retained the day's warmth. There seemed to be nothing I could do to protect myself from the cold, as it would drop to a freezing temperature that night.

Only once before could I remember having to give up, hoping for help to find me. That was during a motorcycle endurance race outside of Webster City, Iowa, when I bashed a tree with my unpadded right shoulder, popping the ball joint out of its socket. Skip Nelson of Webster City found me with my muscle spasm pulling me into a tight ball. Now I needed a friend again, and I didn't trust the Arabs on the other side of the ravine.

The desert was intensely quiet. If there had been a bike engine running within a mile, I could have heard it. My best bet was to disconnect all of the turn signals except one, turn that light on and stand to the left side of the light so the Arabs couldn't see the glow. From it I could pick up a bit of warmth, and it could be seen to the south for a mile or more.

Standing over the light, getting colder as time passed, I started hearing the low, deep tone, the beautiful sound I wanted to hear. Tim Rice, who normally lives in Dearborn, Michigan, pulled up with plenty of gas. Tim wasn't too happy riding back into the desert by himself, especially after a full day in the saddle. I was overjoyed.

After refueling my bike and receiving an extra jacket from Tim, we started riding south again. Within a few miles, I rode into the midst of a group of people and nearly hit the round wall of a mud-bricked cistern that was their town well. I came to a stop totally confused. My front wheel was within a few feet of the community water supply. Tim still was not in the best humor and pulled up to tell me to slow down and follow him. We turned left still unable to see the dark town. Following was the best way to go. Tim had been there before, and soon we were in our own camp.

Camping in nearly freezing temperatures when prepared for the warmth really doesn't compare with the pleasures and comforts of home. But we hadn't chosen home. We chose to deal with what we were served.

In our desert camp, we had no warm campfire to sit around. It was a small gas, single burner fire that couldn't be considered a stove.

I ate quickly, set up my tent and cot, and crawled into my sleeping roll, not to get warm, but to freeze in a more comfortable position. I put on everything I had, including my space blanket, silver side down.

That was another mistake I made that day. Rather than keeping me warm, it condensed my outer body moisture and caused the sleeping bag to become wet from the top down. Lying there freezing, unable to sleep, brought back memories.

When I was sixteen or seventeen years old, one Saturday evening I took a Model A Ford to a bluff overlooking Eagle Lake in North Central Iowa, planning on duck hunting the following day. I didn't know how to hunt ducks or camp in below freezing temperatures, but it certainly seemed as if it would be fun.

During that night, too, I was freezing cold. Also, the bright moon's shining helped to keep me awake. Little did I realize at the time, that the night was a delight compared to what the following day would bring.

Rising before the sun, I went down to the dock and pushed my rented duck boat onto the ice. Duck boats on Eagle Lake had two steel runners, water oars, plus a mud oar as equipment. The mud oar had duck bill shaped paddles on one end and a hardened steel spike with a hook on the other.

There was a channel for a quarter of a mile through eight-foot tall reeds. At the exit was a flag so a hunter could find his way back to shore.

A south wind blew that morning, and by the time the sun was up and shining, I was quite a distance out onto the lake hoping to do some shooting. Far beyond I could see some Canadian geese and open water. Anticipation led me farther and farther as the weather worsened. As the south wind turned eastward, the wind helped push me along. Finally I realized that the open water I was trying to reach was just reflections on the hard, slick, reflective ice and not open water at all.

The ice wasn't thick, but would crack, making me push uphill when the realization came over me that I couldn't get back. The steel spike on the end of the mud oar could only last so long before it finally broke. All I could do was push west and south as much as possible. Only now, with a broken oar, it was slow progress.

I made it to the southwest reaching the high reeds by late afternoon. Out of the wind, I was able to get the boat, still on its ice runners, around the south line of reeds. Finding the red flag ended nearly eighteen hours of misery.

My mind drifted to yet another night when I had lost sleep because of the freezing cold. Northeast of Cartago, Costa Rica, there is a mountain with a huge crater at its summit by the name of Irazu. My wife Jo and I rented an "A" frame cottage high on the mountain so we could get an early start the following morning to explore the crater's interior.

The "A" frame was attractive in its setting but not functional. Wind blew through it. There was no heat except for a small, portable, reflective type electric heater that could easily ignite blankets. So we spent much of the night out of the wind, wrapped in blankets in the bathroom, with the heater in the tub. Joy to the world.

19

We lived through that night. Outside from the high vantage point on the mountain, we saw the sun rise from below the clouds.

We ate and started early, riding up the summit of Mount Irazu and over the ridge of the huge volcanic crater. This was the volcano that a couple in a Cartago restaurant told us about. They said they had never been so horrified as when they were down inside of the crater, so we wanted to experience for ourselves.

Having passed three young men with machetes, there was no way that I would leave either Jo or my bike at the rim. However, the path down into the interior looked like a trail I could ride back up. We snapped a picture from the rim, started the R75/5 BMW and rode the bike down into the crater. Before I parked the bike, I swung it around pointing the bike toward the path up and out. That was only common sense to plot a retreat when feeling insecure.

It was a strange and eerie feeling being down inside a deep cone of rock and ash by ourselves. The only other living thing was Irazu herself letting any intruder know she was still alive by emitting a plume of steam.

Irazu must encompass ten or fifteen acres inside with three smaller craters, plus its big main floor. I was taking pictures of one of the smaller craters, which was steaming slightly, when suddenly the day turned dark. I ran back to Jo and the bike. A total darkness engulfed us. We were horrified, thinking the floor was sinking. The sky above had disappeared. We seemed to be descending deeper into the volcano. We were visualizing falling into the center of the earth. There was no time to think, no time to reason.

I fired up the BMW's engine. With my wife on behind, I started forward, leaving my fingers loose on the grips to keep a straight, forward direction. We hit the trail, but at that high altitude the BMW would hardly climb. I gave the bike full throttle, slipping the clutch, unmercifully trusting the BMW would last to the top. We burst into full sunshine and were able to follow the trail to the rim and over.

The optical illusion was over. A small breeze had whipped a cloud of powder-light ash down upon us. Was it President Franklin D. Roosevelt who told our people, "The only thing we have to fear is fear its self"? Someone was on target.

Looking over to the jeep trail on which we had recently ascended were those three young guys we had seen earlier, this time trying to block our exit no doubt with criminal intent. They didn't succeed!

Spending the night cold and shivering, remembering other cold nights with the very eventful days following, I wondered what the morrow would bring.

By first light of day I crawled with anticipation out of my tent. Standing upright, looking around, seeing for the first time where we had camped, I saw what appeared to be an angel, the symbol of peace and purity. She was an Arabic woman in the morning sun, dressed in her haik, a white shroud–like garment flowing in the North African breeze. I saw her crossing the frost–laced, sandy–loam field.

The warmth of the morning sun warmed my chilled body as a new day began.

IV

THE ARAB – FRIEND OR FOE
25 Degrees North – 4 Degrees East

Motorcycling slowly by myself up a two-hundred-fifty-mile long valley, I passed the valley's most narrow bottleneck, Tadgemout. This is where the French Foreign Legion had built a fort to cut the desert in two trying to subdue the Tuareg, the desert tribesmen, sometime around the turn of the century.

Winding my way up the narrow, twisting valley road, I hadn't seen anyone for what seemed to be hours. It was the usual hot dry afternoon in the North Central Sahara Desert and I was riding a few miles ahead of all the other riders. At that time it seemed a good idea to stop and do some rock climbing. Parking my bike and leaving my camera equipment hanging over my shoulder, I started to climb the south wall of the valley.

The progress upward was a bit difficult because of the steepness, but the old layered stone was firm and easy to grasp. Rather than climbing straight up, I ascended at an angle to the east from where I left my bike. Once I started, I never stopped to look around until I reached a flat outcropping about three hundred feet up and about the same distance down the road from where I left my bike.

The first thing I did was remove the tripod of my camera, pull its three telescoping legs out, and attach the Pentex camera with it's telephoto lens and start looking around. One of the things I wanted to accomplish was to photograph our riders as they came riding down the winding dusty road deep below me in the valley.

Using the telephoto lens as a telescope, I turned the lens toward the east around a bend, which had been out of my line of vision until I was on the rock outcropping. I was eagerly looking for something unusual to photograph when I saw an Arab looking straight up at me. This Arab was not only staring, he was climbing in a straight line toward me.

Quickly I turned the camera away from him, pretending I was photographing rock formations. It was going to take a good ten or fifteen minutes for him to reach me. Behind and below him was a worker boring a hole with a hand auger and parked on the dusty narrow desert floor was his Landrover jeep.

I knew he had noticed me aiming my telephoto lens toward him momentarily, for as soon as our eyes met, my head popped up away from the camera. I swung the camera toward another direction, play acting, using rock formations as my photo subject. I casually watched him approach closer by the minute. Talk about a colorful person! He was a well-dressed gentleman of means. On his head was a gray turban. His blouse had large flowing sleeves and appeared to be made of white silk. Around his waist was a wide, bright red cummerbund. The pants were black, full bloomers, fitting only at the ankle. Rather than wearing the sandals of a Berber, he wore high shoes as black as his trousers.

By watching him climb straight toward me, I could see he was strong and had no qualms about meeting me face to face on this rock canyon wall. Climbing at a steady pace, he didn't seem to be hurrying. I could notice no anger or resentment for pointing my camera toward him. If I had taken his picture or if he thought I had taken his picture, I do not know what mental anguish he would endure because of it. The way I understood it, there would be extreme anxiety if a camera stole his spirit away from his soul. What would the antidote be, smashing my Pentex or seeing my head bounce down the canyon wall unattached from the torso? I couldn't see a weapon hanging from his waist, so I knew a dagger was in place under the full flowing left sleeve of his shining white blouse. It's their way of life. Like American men carrying a billfold in their left hip pocket, the men of the desert carry a dagger up the sleeve above an unclean left hand.

They eat with their right hand; take care of nature with their left. To wave or greet a person with the left hand is as bad as calling another an SOB.

I strongly sensed I had nothing to fear, and I felt no fear. However, I wasn't so naive as to not realize I was trapped. As the last minute of waiting passed, he climbed onto the flat outcropping with me and in his face I perceived a pleasant expression. That is when I flashed my one and only weapon, the weapon that has gotten me through in most trying times, my best smile and hello.

His reply was in English. He never looked at the camera, nor mentioned its existence. In fact, he never asked me anything about myself, but in turn, I was interested in what he was doing out here so far from anything.

This is what he told me. They (Algeria) would like to continue the road from Ain Salah to Tamanrasset by constructing it three meters wide. Then if and when money was available, and if needed, the road would be widened to six meters. Our conversation was never social nor personal, but totally on road configuration.

There is a road bed of stones fitted together and up about five feet above sand level for ten or fifteen miles south on Ain Salah. When President Charles de Gaulle told the people of France, "It's time to give Algeria back to the Algerians," not only did the French Foreign Legion leave this mostly desert country, but the construction companies left also.

To build a road for five hundred sixty–five miles in heat and moving sand would be an engineering achievement. The sand is old and has been tumbled for tens of thousands of years. This makes the granules so smooth that concrete will not adhere to it. Water is something you only see in flat broad pools, always just a few hundred feet beyond reaching.

The construction equipment that I had seen for the past one thousand miles consisted of one sandplow on the front of a truck and this gentleman's hand auger that couldn't bring samples up out of the sand. By himself it would take years of sample gathering and recording

24

necessary information before a road could even be put on the drawing board.

After an exceedingly enjoyable visit, we heard the low drone of a Honda four stroke motorcycle approaching from the northwest coming down the long narrow canyon. Then a thick column of dust could be seen before Tim Rice pulled up and stopped next to my bike.

It was time for both of us to leave. Not shaking hands or bidding a farewell, we just started climbing down, the Arab to the right and I to the left. Never taking a picture, I just put my tripod and camera in the case so as not to offend the colorful Algerian.

Days later, in the desert city of Tamanrasset in the center of the Sahara, I walked into a room where food was served on long narrow tables. As I stepped in, I met the Arab of the desert face to face. Our eyes met. There was a flash of pleasant recognition; his eyes fell and his facial expression flattened. Our paths crossed as strangers.

Travellers via the Great South from El Golea and at every following step you should state at the Daira your arrival and your departure. You will be provided with travelling permit. Any infraction of this rule is punished by law Your security and your life depende on this.

V

THE VALLEY OF THE ATOM BOMBS
24 Degrees North – 4 Degrees East

Looking off to the west, I could see a steel tower rising above a line of foothills. Stopping to get a better look, I realized there was only one reason on earth why a steel tower would be built out in the Sahara Desert beyond this row of foothills.

This I had to go see and I knew who would go with me, tall wiry Barney Coskie. He carried a bible in his hip pocket, and that bible was a book by Zane Gray. He read and lived the adventures of the Old West.

Barney did not wear a Belstaff all–weather, off–road riding suit.   Rather, he wore hand–rubbed, rawhide leather pants and coat which he, no doubt, cut and stitched himself.   Around his waist was a broad, natural–colored, leather belt with a sheathed foot–long knife, both his own creations. I never saw him sit down to eat or visit. Barney's regular stance was leaning against anything handy while standing on one foot. As he read, he relived a life he missed by a hundred years.

When Barnie stopped, I pointed out the tower showing above the first row of hills with a low range of mountains behind. "Barnie," I said, "this has to be where the French tested their atomic bombs. Let's take a look."

We made arrangements with Ralph Hurtienne, Barnie's riding partner that day, to leave a torch burning on a high ridge for us late that night so we could find our camp. We would be there a few hours late depending how long it would take us to explore.

Barnie and I rode our motorcycles west across the desert until we reached the foothills. There was no way to cross these rough little mountains, but I was sure we could flank the south end and find the entrance to the valley. Going south, in just a few miles the hills flattened and we were able to circumvent to the west. Then we turned back north into a valley that was just a few hundred feet wide.

Going over and through, we were able to pass the barbed wire entanglements. As we continued north up the ravine, we saw two small metal buildings and rode over, scanning the interior in curious disbelief.

My first reaction was a stunned stare, seeing first hand what a slow, methodical destruction exposure to atomic radiation had inflicted upon the building and its contents. The buildings were, or had been, galvanized tin sheds about twenty feet square with horizontal panels that swung up like an old–fashioned chicken house. The metal had a thick corrosive build–up leaving it green and yellow from atomic radiation. Looking inside, we saw that the buildings' transformers and other old electrical devices were also discolored in yellow and green from atomic exposure.

After walking around in curious dismay, seeing what radiation had done to the equipment and buildings, we started our bikes and continued on north up the valley. We crossed over a steel arched bridge that spanned an eroded ravine. This structure had open side rails and a width adequate for trucks; however, it was bent, not from overload, but bent upward from distortion.

A quarter mile later we saw another bridge crossing a small gorge. This bridge was twisted much worse than the first. Again it wasn't bent down, but up. The west side of the north end of this entirely steel structure was raised up three or four feet and twisted thirty or forty degrees. It was evident that we were getting nearer to the location of where a nuclear bomb had been detonated, as only tremendous heat with the force of unimaginable wind could have blown away the approach to the bridge and bent it upwards.

Crossing the bridge, one of us, then the other dropped down the north end that had no approach. We knew the return wouldn't be easy. We stopped to visit and

27

replenish a bit of our body fluids with a couple of swallows from our canteens. We didn't visit about what the forces of an atomic bomb had done but rather about the year of the occurrence.

We weren't so ignorant of the fact that we didn't know we were walking and riding on radioactive fire. When, was the key. It never rains to wash or carry away the radiation. What gave us some sense of security were the windstorms of the desert valley. They may have exchanged the surface sand. Only time can cool the radiation from the rock and metal. It was our hope that by this December, 1974, enough time had elapsed to reduce dangerous radiation. We certainly didn't want to ride into camp later that night glowing like a pair of incandescent light bulbs.

This was a once in a lifetime opportunity to view the aftermath of a weapon that changed the political structure of the planet Earth for generations to come and may possibly cause the "homo sapiens" to join the dinosaurs.

Just by looking, there wasn't any evidence left as to where point zero was, inasmuch as if towers were used above the valley floor; they may have been vaporized and the crater below filled by the natural movement of the desert sand. However, on the valley's western mountainside, solid granite was splintered like a baseball's shattering an automobile windshield. This we found twice nearer the north end and the widest part of the valley.

Because of the low mountains to the west, it became dark quickly as the sun set, leaving us to find our way out only by our headlights and the ability of our bikes to handle the soft sand.

We didn't consider going back south the way we came in, thinking it would not only be difficult to find the bridges, but treacherous to cross with only headlights not to mention the difficulty of getting onto the bridge from the north end that was twisted upward and without an approach. Then too, we had to ride past the tributaries from the gorge and the debris that was scattered and never retrieved after the blast.

We rode north into the unknown. But that is what explorers love most, the unknown. In just three or four miles we encountered barbed wire entanglements that were in such disarray from the bomb's wind blast that we had to repeatedly probe to find a way through. As on the south entrance to the valley, there were many rows of the barbed wire spirals. On the north they were in line of sight, getting a direct hit from the blast, leaving them in a tangled mess. It may have been easier to find a way through on foot. In the darkness we had to stay in the saddle going back and forth using our headlights looking for holes through which to cross. After a few minutes of winding through this maze, we rode through the last barbed wire.

Even with all the turning and backing around in the dark moonless night, we found our directions easily by lining up with recognizable heavenly constellations. The route to find our camp was east into the flat land, then due south.

After a few good hours of riding, we saw, off to the right, the torch Ralph had lit for us. By then it was past 2:00 a.m. and all were asleep. One of my buddies had set up my tent so the only evening chore was to clean the Honda's air cleaner, eat a food bar and go to sleep. Barnie never used a tent. He would take a six by six-foot tarp, hold two corners with outstretched arms as he stood, then pull one end around his shoulders with his left hand. He kept the right hand out, holding the tarpaulin tight. Then, using his feet, he made himself twirl, landing in the sand. Where he stopped rolling was where Barney slept.

VI

DUCT TAPE
23 Degrees North – 5 Degrees East

There is no outer limit to the judicial boundaries encompassing the influence of Murphy's Law. Our cook was piloting the sands of the Sahara with no apparent respect for Murphy's authority. It was poor judgment to throttle up hard, facing the glare of the desert's late morning sun.

I was riding behind and to his right, when he dropped out of sight without returning to view. The wind had whipped a long, narrow sand depression leaving a few gallon-size boulders exposed. One of these rocks made a base for a thigh sandwich topped off with a well–placed Honda XL250.

I left my bike on a knoll and walked back thinking to myself, this will be the longest day. If all you could see were the cook's boots, you wouldn't have known whether he was coming or going. From the waist up all seemed okay except for his twisted face and foul language. I brought over both of our canteens and life support foods in the pockets of my Belstaff riding suit. Then I sat down to hold and comfort him as much as possible.

Even though he was our cook, he was still a human being. The only thing worse than his language was his cooking. He could take absolutely atrocious food and turn it into something unfit for human consumption. Remember the laughing hyena? That was our cook, laughing while destroying our body's digestive system.

Every coin has two sides. On the other side was a man who knew he was in grave peril. His thigh was not broken; it was crushed. All I could do was hold, comfort and listen. I listened to him explain to me how he would prevent himself from going into shock. He remained positive, calm and alert by carrying on a conversation.

30

Minutes turned into hours as we lay in the sand of the Sahara. God did but few people favors when he created Africa. The inhabitants have had to either succumb to or endure atrocities from within and those brought by others to their continent, enduring diseases and an unforgiving climate. For us the time spent there was a small favor, such as it was. We were at the northwestern edge of the Highlands of the Hoggar, which is considered near the center of the Sahara Desert. The heat is not as intense and there is scrub brush nearby. If this situation had occurred any previous day, the heat from the sand with radiant heat from the sun would have cooked us both.

At last help had arrived. A "stretched" Landrover pulled up and stopped just a few hundred feet away to the east. Looking down the narrow depression toward us were eight uniformed, darkly tanned soldiers. They must have been from Fort Laperrine in Tamanrasset which was only a few hours away. There was no place else within a hundred miles for them to have come from.

Five, ten, fifteen minutes went by. I could hear the engine running. I was looking at them, and they were looking at us.

They didn't seem to be talking to each other and I didn't see a radio antenna. At first I thought they would come to help. Then I started to wonder if they would rob us, but I could see they weren't making plans. Approximately fifteen minutes went by when the driver put the Landrover in gear and disappeared from my sight and they were gone.

I was back to listening to the cook's rambling speech. He was an airline pilot telling me about the Northern lights and the beauty of the flashing, colorful Auroras in the night flights across Canada.

Sitting there in the heat and blinding sun, I must have been out of it for a while. I didn't hear anything. But looking over my right shoulder to the South, on the ridge next to my bike, I saw our support truck and three of our XL250 riders.

Like the Genie that was released from the bottle after a millennium of time, I didn't know whether to be mad or glad, glad because I was finally released or mad because it took them so long to find us.

With numbed senses, I kept holding the injured cook as our riders began turning him into a cocoon. Using a sixty-yard roll of duct tape and sticks made from the thorn bushes, they started to work.

Leaving his riding suit on and not moving his legs from the position I was holding them in, he soon took the form of a silver-gray mummy as they placed sticks against his legs and wrapped duct tape around and around until they were but one extension.

The body was done the same, alternating sticks and duct tape, tying his torso to his hips with so many cut sticks that they resembled the barrels of a Gatling gun. There was no need to leave an area for him to relieve himself. That is usually taken care of by dehydration of the body in the dry, hot Sahara.

Then we had to get him loaded. Loading was accomplished by picking him up out of the sand like a tapered log, then carrying him up to the truck and placing him on the tailgate. Lying on the tailgate was the last semblance of peace this man of misery would even approach until the sun again rose above the eastern sands.

Pads were put down on the four square, two-hundred-gallon gasoline containers, which was the only level area on top of the support truck. It may seem cruel, but we had no choice except to put him on top alone so he could use his two good hands to keep himself from bouncing off the truck.

The thirty or forty miles south into Tamanrasset would take three or four hours traveling ten to fourteen miles per hour over the ripples of the ever moving desert sand. On our XL250 Hondas it was a piece of cake, but for Afro Annie, the support truck, and its rooftop rider, it was not. The ride consisted of bumps eighteen inches forward, four inches down and four inches upward. That's three thousand five hundred twenty bumps per mile, or some one hundred twenty–five thousand sand ripples before arriving in Tamanrasset. Tamanrasset wouldn't be heaven, just a sedative, getting out of the cocoon to a splint, then back into the desert.

Heat and sandals apparently do not damage streets. As we rolled into Tamanrasset the streets were sandy and smooth. As always, we went to the fort first to let the Deira know we were in town, got our passports stamped and gave them the required information. We proceeded to the hospital where we unloaded the dust covered, duct-taped refugee suffering from a trap set by the winds and the shifting sand.

Entering the local hospital was just a matter of opening the door to a one–story building of rooms and hallways. That's all it was, rooms and hallways, without furniture or people. The only things left were the mattresses. No doubt the reason for leaving them is they had been gaining in weight through use. Their last patient, which we were just now bringing in, was no example of sanitation himself, an unbathed, duct–taped cocoon caked with desert dust.

Looking back as I left, I could see similarities between the mattress and the victim. Both lay flat and motionless, but one had yellow stains. As for me, I thought that was the last time I would play mister nice guy to a cook whom the riders had learned to hate through eating.

After leaving the hospital we rode into an unanticipated Continental surprise party. The hotel we rode into was about a half block square with a wooden fence and one-room huts around the outside perimeter, leaving the center clear. However, this evening it was not empty. Rather, in the center sat a German built Mercedes Unitog camper truck with a sealed teardrop shaped motorcycle trailer.

Who greeted us in complete disbelief this December, 1974, evening in Tamanrasset, Algeria, but Mr. Clean's Yamaha of Europe, with American Hot Dog desert riders and their high tech support crew.

It must have blown their minds when the nine of us came riding in out of the desert resembling "WW II's Battered Bastards of Bastogne." We hadn't been under a roof for two or three weeks, unwashed for lack of water for days and sleeping next to our motorcycles by night.

By contrast, they looked like they had just departed from Mel's Diner. All were well fed and casually dressed.

We didn't get into deep conversation. They were on a publicity seeking adventure with two TV cameramen, hoping to show a great adventure of Yamaha's DT360 motorcycles crossing the Sahara Desert on ABC's *Wide World of Sports*. Rather than seeing a dirt bike jumping sand dunes, it would be interesting for ABC to show the real high-tech Mercedes Unitog in the desert just to see what tens of thousands of Deutshe Marks can produce. This very specialized four-wheel desert vehicle does not have conventional axles per se, but has each wheel independently suspended like a motorcycle or an airplane landing gear giving it excellent ground clearance and suspension.

A year or so later I received a letter from Yamaha USA answering my inquiry, stating their trip was not completed. This I can understand, as North Africa is a piece of cake compared to the Southern Sahara.

After our short visit, I purchased a bucket of water and went to a booth where, with the use of one bucket of water, I was like a new man.

Clean and skinny from dehydration, not enough food and long hours of riding, it felt good to sit at a table, a first since Ceuta, Spain, for a real meal. After eating, I walked to my cot for what I thought would be a long and restful sleep. During the night, Yamaha of Europe pulled out. Tamanrasset may have been where they threw in the towel for we never saw a tire track south.

"Afro Trek, on your feet! Afro Trek, on your feet," shouted Bill Record. We had to get out to the airstrip.

Two of us landed on our feet ready for work. Apparently there are at least two groups for whom it is difficult to get volunteers to give assistance, gays and lousy cooks. Our patient fit the latter.

If strangers hadn't carried me in for doctors to reconstruct the results of my shortcomings, this body of mine would already have completed its life cycle. Maybe I felt an obligation to the human race, who knows? But there I went again. Barnie Costkie and I unloaded the trailer that would be used as an ambulance. Bill Record and Jack Hawthorn had been up all night working with and for our cook.

Bill managed to get a plane to come out this night. It would land about four a.m. and would take off at four-thirty a.m. with or without our patient. Because of the intense heat, planes would only land or take off at night.

We climbed into the trailer for our ride to the hospital. It became easy to understand why livestock do not enjoy traveling.

Going inside to get our patient, we found him out of his duct tape and lying on a stretcher with his leg straight and secured. Picking him up I made the second poor judgment. The first mistake was coming on this airport trip. The secondly, I was picking up the heavy end of the stretcher and my end went on first nearest Afro Annie's exhaust fumes.

Setting the handles of the stretcher on the front board of the trailer, we started out of town. Tamanrasset was dark at night with only a very few lights in the business district.

At the edge of town where the street ends, the sand ripples began. We picked up the litter by the grips, holding it to keep the bumps from pounding this prostrate figure into unbearable pain. We had to maintain this position for at least an hour.

I squatted to get the pressure off my arms, trying to alleviate my own problems by reliving my enshrined memories of long distance off-road endurance races. I was remembering racing over the corduroy roads in Michigan's five hundred mile Jack Pine endurance races, transgressing between the rails on old railroads of the Midwest and the sand ripples here in the Sahara.

To make life more bearable, why don't the logs, railroad ties and ripples run length ways? Even in this darkness, I could still see stopped competition riders on the corduroy roads bent over their gas tanks in near fetal positions, motionless and exhausted. The only thing that runs length ways are the ruts, the endless ruts of Michigan's mud trails. These twin trenches were possibly made by wagons and deepened by Jeeps. They had a crown in the center that was wet, slick and grassy.

Riding at speed on the crown is not only risky but foolhardy. Dropping into the deep, narrow rut is no better. My big 500 four–stroke motorcycle of yesteryear was responsive and forgiving, but to go miles at speed in a six inch wide trench is a matter of attitude and discipline. At times the thought would pass through my mind of wishing I'd go ahead and crash and get it over with.

Negative thoughts came and went. With the negative thought going, I renewed my discipline by bringing my hands, arms and body loose. I kept the power smooth, riding only for now. The rut was reduced from miles to the distance I was looking.

That which has a beginning likewise has an ending. Reminiscing with intense concentration, the hour-plus drive was over.

Unable to see in the moonless night, the intense bumping turned into a smooth airport runway. Relief came to our cramped arms and legs as we set our silent victim down on the trailer floor.

To our left was a big tail dragger, twin engine commercial airliner, with its inside lights on. Beyond were two hangers. That's about all I could see as I walked a few steps, getting my legs and arms back to normal.

About twelve feet in the air, a rubber-tired loading ramp was leaning against an open doorway on the co–pilot side near the nose of the aircraft. The five seats directly behind the co–pilot and the partition were removed to accommodate the stretcher. Apparently the crew was emphatic about getting our wounded rider on board as there were neither greetings nor conversation, just direction to start him up the ramp.

If the crew didn't know, they should have realized how unstable this tall, two–rubber–tired loading ramp was. Rather than keeping help on the bottom side, Record and Hawthorn went up into the nose cabin with the crew to receive the stretcher case, while Barnie and I pushed our patient up the long narrow suitcase ramp.

After Barnie and I got him on the incline, we moved him up, stretcher and all, feet first, one of us on each side. We reached my limit as I'm much shorter than six-foot four-inch Barnie. So I got on the ramp underneath and started pushing up as I climbed, inching upwards. As I got over the fulcrum point of the teeter-totter type ramp, with assistants leaning out the door and down the ramp, they got hold of our cook by the ankles and started pulling him up. I kept on climbing and pushing the stretcher above me.

Then it happened. All of our weight was on the unblocked airplane side of the ramp's tires. They rolled back, dumping the ramp upside down, and I landed headfirst but easy, hanging on as I went down. The ramp rolled away!

Our wounded cook with his crushed thigh was close enough to the door that the assistant hung onto him by his ankles as he hung straight down screaming in hysterical agony. Barnie was able to get under and at least touch our patient's head with his fingertips. His frantic screaming went unheard into the dark, still desert night as two from the plane came jumping and sliding down the ladder from the other side of the aircraft to help me push the ramp back up before the cook would drop straight down on his head to sure death.

Barnie had to leave all the holding to the guy at the door as we brought the ramp under him. Now, at least, he was at a forty–five-degree angle. I started backup the incline to again assist getting the poor fellow into the aircraft. This time, however, men were down at the bottom holding weight on the outside end as should have been done on the first try. There were two men left inside the airliner to receive the victim as I helped by pushing him stretcher and all from the firmly held ramp.

There's a limit to the length of time a person can scream. Hanging head down, the cook reached his limit. Barnie helped me get the stretcher rearranged and at last we got the poor fellow inside.

Jack Hawthorn accompanied our brave, fallen rider as the doors closed and the engines started. We rolled the ill fated incline plane back as the big tail dragger revved its twin engines, released its brakes, moving straight ahead, never turning but lifting off into the desert darkness.

Bill Record drove by himself on the return trip to Tamanrasset. Barnie and I preferred riding in the trailer. I sat on my haunches, holding onto a sideboard, not wanting to see or talk after the trauma. I preferred, rather, to mentally review the past twenty–four hours.

I vividly saw another of life's dramas in my mind again. I realized our ex–cook could still die of shock on this mercy flight out. His every minute must have been hell. But on the positive side, he quit using foul language and never once complained.

The continuous pounding from the sand ripples propelled through our squatted legs as the eastern horizon relinquished its first blush of dawn. I may have become tranquil in thought, enshrining in memory the simple things a dirt rider appreciates most, good suspension, a responsive throttle and duct tape.

The author; Photo by David Ray in the Sahara crossing: Whatever one imagines the Sahara to be, he is correct. It is so huge, that every desert condition exists.

A Tuareg chieftain views my cycle and I acknowledge
his camel as two cultures pass in the desert.

Photo by Bill Record: A rare and unusual photograph
of an unveiled Tuareg.

VII

A GEOMETRIC SOLUTION
22 Degrees North – 6 Degrees East

I had been following the desert markers a few hundred feet to their left. All the other riders were doing the same except to their right. The problem started because another line of markers intersected the first line we were following at an angle from the left.

Far to the south was an irregular, nearly black ridge descending over the horizon. I was getting farther away from the ridge as I angled northeast. There were scores of small hills between me and the dark ridge. These hills were low, maybe fifteen feet in height, and their shape was similar to half grapefruits; however, the riding surface was smooth unspoiled gravel. Not seeing my fellow riders, I decided it was time to reconnoiter before motoring too far north. Stopping at one of the hills, I took my binoculars and see-through compass to the summit for a visual sighting. Someone was lost.

I looked south with the binoculars and slowly moved the sighting west. Finally I saw dust moving east. There was no way of estimating the distance, but I was pretty sure of the rider's speed after days of riding together.

By seeing his dust, knowing his speed and using the ridge in the background as an identification, I had all the information I needed to formulate a right triangle to intersect with the dust of the rider.

Using the see-through compass, I marked a slight depression on the dark ridge perpendicular from where I was standing. Then I subtracted forty–five degrees and moved the compass to the left until the reading was the subtracted number I needed. Using the compass body as

41

a sighting device without moving it, I was able to visually mark an unforgettable bump on the dark south ridge.

I put my compass away and waited with the binoculars focused on the light tan dust approaching the perpendicular line. When the telltale dust was nearly there, I dropped the binoculars in their case while I ran down the hill. My trusty bike started on the first kick. I headed for the forty–five–degree markers on the ridge. I calculated twenty–five miles per hour multiplied by 1.4 and added three miles per hour to make up for crooked lines because of the hills coming up with thirty–eight miles per hour.

Standing on the foot pegs, knees firm against the tank, I let the bike do the work at thirty–eight miles per hour. There was some anticipation on my part as the minutes passed. When the bike crossed in front of me with a light tan plumage of dust, I turned left behind the rider that I had monitored. No one ever discovered that I had been lost. Substituting speed for distance in a right triangle is not a calculation taught in the classroom. However, the formula and accuracy was so precisely correct that afternoon in the Sahara that even Pythagoras would have been pleased.

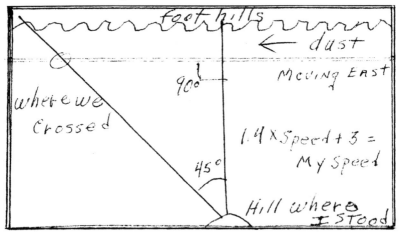

A simple application of geometry united me with the other riders.

VIII

LOST IN THE SOUTHERN SAHARA
21 Degrees North – 6 Degrees East
to 19 Degrees North - 7 Degrees East

While camping in a half–mile wide desert valley, we found nearly twenty round tennis ball size objects that had been brought in by the winds. We took one and opened it, having no idea what we'd find. The shell was thin to give it lightness. Inside there were seeds similar to those of a tomato with white threads that at one time had been foam. What wind could have brought and kept them so close together after hundreds of miles? None of us had a clue.

Soon after first light of our new day, we were breaking camp and climbing the steep ascent at the valley's end. It was evident the desert wind had cut through the surface rock, then with its relentless blowing had cut deep into the desert floor creating this valley, leaving pyramids of stone as high as the upper walls of the valley.

Rather than hitting the rocky ascent at full throttle with all of its ramifications, we "Z"ed the escarpment. On reaching the top and riding to the right, we found foundations of a few buildings or fortifications. It was probably built during the last few hundred years for protection from the winds or from a forthcoming confrontation. These surely couldn't have been for living as there hadn't been life or water here for thousands of years and there was no indication of a roof. However, looking down the valley, with the sun to our backs, given the location's many advantages (except for the hostile environment), one could see for miles.

Our last desert marker was still in the valley casting its long shadow from the early morning sun. The markers are usually a column of stones about three feet high that have been used for as long as caravans have crossed the desert. They mark a trail or a path through the desert. When going was good, we would see one every five or six miles. There were two riders ahead of us, and the rest would start in pairs as they finished breaking camp. Pettyjohn was my buddy rider this day. We rode on as nearly as we could keeping in line with the previous marker.

Our last desert marker was still in the valley, casting its long shadow from the early morning sun.

Going east from the marker up the escarpment from the valley's end, we entered the darkness of a high, brown

44

desert. Even using the best of our judgment, we became separated and lost from each other, wasting a day's worth of irreplaceable water.

Pettyjohn and I rode eastward for a few miles, then stopped where the high desert dropped into low, soft-sand lowlands. With no tracks beyond, we turned to zero on the compass going due north down and across a steep ravine, climbing up to the high desert as before. Just as soon as we made our first turn, I started recording distance and compass readings on my Norelco recorder. In the event we would become hopelessly lost, we would be able to backtrack to the valley ridge just above where we camped, hoping others would do the same. I've never tried backtracking using only the odometer and compass, but I did realize we would have but one try at making it. Would the others be able to backtrack without the help of the tracking sand?

This was the most unusual terrain I had ever known or heard about. Of course, the rock is trackless, but the rock is so dull and porous, it absorbs the light from the sun. The soft, brown, porous, volcanic rock so completely consumed the light from the sun that only the dusty chrome rims of Pettyjohn's Honda were readily visible when his bike was nearby.

Continuing north, we encountered yet another ravine excavated by the centuries of westerly winds. Going on but a few hundred more yards north we stopped. To go on was like entering infinity, with a dry atmosphere, dusty looking above the horizon and the never-ending darkness below. Voicing the odometer and new compass reading of ninety degrees into the Norelco, we made our right turn again to the east. Within a few miles we dropped from the high, brown desert into a broad sand depression where the heat was entrapped. Our bellies were slightly tight with the realization we could have been lost in what might be the hottest hell- hole on earth. Life here could not be maintained for long because of the intense heat and also the excessive glare of the sun.

There were no tracks except for the pair we were making. Instead, we saw the largest, most extensive vertical mirage conceivable.

Imagine yourself sitting in the center of a large theater with a one-hundred-twenty degree wide stage. The curtains are closed and gently moving back and forth. Now turn up the lights and turn up the heat and just in front of you is the likeness of a vertical mirage. Anything you are looking for in there can be seen.

An off-colored stone will be magnified by the glare of the sun and may look to you as anything unexpected or recognizable and can start a chase as fruitless as a dog chasing its own tail. If the sun has gotten to you and you are not reasoning your thoughts, the ever- moving image may resemble your buddy, even though he is behind you. In a moment of panic, you move toward what you think is your companion. As you move, the image moves. Moving more, you become fearful that he is leaving you. You give chase — into the endless desert, reaching, striving, expanding your body until the chase is ended by the solar's relentless fury. The image departs with the resting sun. The victim remains forevermore, leaving his tracks to be erased by the shifting sand, his body the beginning of another drift.

To prevent this scenario, we tried to ignore the beckoning, tormenting mirage. Finding nothing but the mirage that was immediately before us, we continued onward to an even odometer mileage where we stopped. We recorded the compass and odometer readings, added forty-five degrees to our ninety degrees on the compass, putting us now at southeast, one hundred thirty-five degrees. Soon we came upon a motorcycle tire track that had been made in a large curve. Thinking one of our riders went out into an ever enlarging spiral, we left our one hundred thirty-five degree route and bisected this rider's curve, believing in the center would be one or more of our group. Whoever made the circle did a nearly perfect turn. In less than a mile, the mirage just to the right of center turned black, went wild and shot up hundreds of feet. Baby, we weren't home but six of us were together.

46

There was no celebration as Don Murk, Bernie Coskie and Ross Swanson were still out there and, like us, hadn't been seen since the ruins up on the ridge where we had camped the night before. They had stopped to look for artifacts, expecting to catch up soon.

By now it was nearly two o'clock and as previously agreed upon, at an even hour we would burn a tire as a smoke signal to help a lost rider to find us. What a waste! The tire soaked with oil and gasoline burned well with plenty of black smoke. However, with the concentration of intense heat in this depression, the smoke wouldn't rise. All it did was make a black surface of thick smoke less than chest high. It looked solid enough to support a motorcycle helmet.

This smoke signal didn't work. We knew our men would be searching for us, and our hopes were that the lost riders would find our tracks. If they would cross a ridge north and go east, they would be sure to see tracks. Our only option was to stay out of the sun and off the burning sand while waiting for the darkness of the evening, enabling all of our riders to see.

We were waiting and contemplating, thinking of what we were going to do if we couldn't find the lost riders tonight. There was no answer; nothing we could do would be fair. We most likely were going to run out of water before arriving at the next well. There wasn't any room for extra water reserve as we needed every spare container space for the eight hundred miles of travel between gasoline replenishments. Thoughts of ourselves and families diminished as we tried to surmise what might have happened out there.

As a boy, my mother told me, "An idle mind is a devil's playground."

In this idleness, pondering the inevitable, a person tries to reason whether the devil is at play justifying any decision as long as there's logic. Or, is God's will being considered? What is the right thing to do? Or being personally selfish, would it be easier giving up by looking for them until our water was gone and then to succumb? Or should we go on, and during the quietness of my remaining years, in the inevitable flashbacks, would I see their undisturbed bones and bikes making their last contribution as a mirage's dancing reflection? Or would I see them trying to weigh the odds of ending up hopelessly disoriented on the high plateau?

If not found during the forthcoming darkness, decision time would arrive before dawn. Should we stay and keep looking with no one getting out alive, or should we abandon the three to sure death by themselves so that the rest of us could survive?

Lost in an area is one thing, but misjudging south as we did north might be an irreversible error. The reason Pettyjohn and I chose north was that it looked better than south, even without finding the next desert marker. I was the only one who didn't have his hand-held recorder destroyed by the Moroccans, as they thought it was part of my camera outfit. It gave me a feeling of security navigating this day. Each of the missing riders had adequate skills, but there is always the possibility of an unexpected occurrence, then what?

By late afternoon, the sun had lost its violent intensity and we could see to the south.

Getting the binoculars, I rode over to a stone hill shaped like a walnut half shell. Climbing to its summit on foot, I searched as far as I could to no avail. When I returned, Sherm Cooper and Bill Record were preparing to ride southwest to a high ridge.

Plainly visible, just a few miles away, was an access to the summit, which looked to be near a yellow line of sand. The summit would give a view to the desert beyond. They left using hard throttles after the decision to explore beyond the ridge. Within the hour they were back with no sightings of our missing riders, but with a story of another thrilling escape.

Going up the north wall of the high ridge, using full throttle, the firm sand ended. When Cooper and Record encountered 'fall sand' (sand that has been dropped by the wind within the last one or two years) at the summit, both men flew over the handlebars as their bikes stuck upright in the soft fall sand. Their vision had been impaired by riding into the sunset and by the rest of the summit. The lives of the surprised riders were saved because of the soft sand stopping their bikes within a few feet of dropping over a four hundred-foot cliff! The rolling fall sand would have rolled with the pair to surely smother out their lives.

"That's it. That's all for now," Bill Record told us after returning. "We'll wait until after the evening glow. It's going to be a moonless night. Our headlights should help locate that wandering trio."

For the next two hours we were topping our gas tanks, eating some bread with apricot jam and drinking a cup of freshly brewed coffee. It restrained us from leaving for those two hours after sunset. But with the evening glow in the same direction we would be searching, it was necessary to get maximum beacon effect from our headlights if we were to locate each other in this endless desert wasteland.

Two of our riders started west across a few miles of sand, then up into the trackless high desert of brown volcanic stone. To keep from becoming completely disoriented up there at night, they stopped and read the stars that they could recognize, the celestial markers that never change.

Thirty minutes passed in the completely dark night. Then, high on the western plateau, coming down into the low desert, were five headlights, and all were approaching at a good speed.

With the sight of all five fast moving headlights, it was evident that all our men were healthy and the unanswerable questions would never have to be answered or discussed.

By the time the hunters and the hunted pulled into camp, the rest of us were loaded, engines running and starting to pull out. The decision had already been made to ride east, the only logical direction as south was blocked by a high ridge with an impossible descent beyond the crest.

We spread out into a wide sweep. The sand was rather firm with no ripples, making for miles of good riding, a perfect night for dirt biking. Riding east, there was virtually no way of hitting anything or dropping off as the westerly winds deposit their sands to the east. About midnight, we rode into a community of sandstone towers and had to stop because of the pending confusion.

In first light, after camping for the last hours of the night, we could see a multitude of sandstone columns, still growing taller from the wind whipping the desert floor deeper as centuries pass.

Everyone broke camp early and left, except for Don Murk, Sherm Cooper and myself. Rather than continuing on, we stayed and rode through where no life of any kind may have ever been. Only a good dirt bike could roam over these rolling sand dunes within this valley of nature's artistic splendor.

I still remember the thrill of the ride and of the sight of what was yet being created by the westerly winds and the kept secret for nothing to share. There were thousands of acres of these columns, so many you couldn't see beyond the next one, looking as though each was carved by a different touch.

As in anything, there is an end. The end came at a high desert plateau. Above and to the southwest was a wall of vertical sandstone with a ramp up the side. If I would approach this ramp of sand straight toward the wall, then bend a hard left hitting the steep grade with my engine singing in second gear, I could fly over the top to another unforgettable view, or I could become buried in rolling sand. I cared not where I would be buried, but I wasn't ready for my final resting place on that particular day and certainly not while I was alive. I stopped and used my Pentex 35mm on what might have been. Then I restarted my faithful bike, made a one hundred eighty degree turn and retraced my sand tracks to find my two friends.

An hour or two behind, using sand tracks as our direction finder, we left this magnificent park which is visited only by the sun and occasional sporadic winds, taking with us our memories and leaving only our tracks, tracks to be erased by shifting sands but never to be crossed.

50

Following the tracks southeast, the sand finally ended and we entered miles of flat, smooth, hard–packed pea gravel that looked to be cemented by nature. The distance one could see was limited only by dimension.

On the other side of these flats, we found tracks in the sand made by our comrades, still going southeast. Following the tracks until nearly noon, we rode up a large arch–shaped sand dune. In the bowl below was an old walled town surrounded by eight or ten-foot-high walls. There were only a few roofs showing, as it was completely blown full of sand.

Just north a few hundred feet were stone homes where robed people were coming out to meet our support truck and other riders were stopped nearby.

Another half-mile east was a very small fort and the border crossing leaving Algeria and entering Niger. There must have been a low volume well, chances being the only well at the fort. These people, no doubt, spend their days in the one-room homes to keep out of the sun and off the burning sand. I don't know why or how they live.

At some time in the past, there may have been trade to the south with the city of Aggaden only two hundred miles to the east. However, this had been cut off in recent years by sand dunes forming between the towns. These dunes were some sixty miles wide and four hundred fifty miles long.

Crossing into Niger was a beginning of thirty miles of sand dunes. It was a piece of cake for the bikes. For our support truck, Afro Annie, it was a matter of very careful driving, to avoid being trapped between tails of sand dunes or going into the pits where the sand had been wiped out by the winds. Afro Annie a Dodge Power Wagon had been bought in Manchester, New York, by Bill Record.

When our Afro Annie leaned heavily to one side, all of the weight would transfer to the sidewalls of the down-side tires. Time and again she tipped to the critical point while transversing low spots or softer sand on one side. Its near limit was reached after driving off the end of the sand ladders directly into a small depression. These sand

51

ladders were made of steel angle iron and about eight-foot in length. We used them as a steel track to drive on while in soft sand.

Just as I was dragging one of the ladders near the left rear corner, there was a loud explosion blowing sand in my face and talc all over the inside wheel well and running gear turning the metal white as from frost. For a few minutes I couldn't see what had happened.

The wheel had broken under at the lug bolts, breaking completely into the outer rim, exposing the innertube, which blew inward, discharging its powdery contents of talcum powder.

The front end was up at an angle with the left rear sitting on what was left of a wheel and the axle housing. It was now shovel time, time to start digging out from the high side to level the vehicle before she tipped on over. If we would lose our mother ship, we would lose it all.

A few good men in the soft sand and the heat of the day started digging, blocking, and jacking up tons of our truck back to its equilibrium. There was no conversation. We worked on our knees, digging and blocking until we were able to replace the broken wheel with a spare. Then we dug a trench to slide a sand ladder under the wheel to let the truck down on. With the steel ladder in place under the low side, we were ready to give her a try. Bill started the engine as we stepped back to watch the Dodge Power Wagon climb up and out.

Sand laddering had become a way of progress. When forward motion ended, we dug sand away from the front wheels, standing the ladders in the holes we dug against the tires. Bill Record put the Dodge in low side and let the tires grip the ladder's crossbars. While giving the truck a fast idle, it lifted itself out of the holes. As the ladders dropped forward, he would ride the length of the ladders and off the end until stuck again, only to repeat the process over and over until new, firm sand was found.

While Afro Annie got a rest from plowing and hard pulling, we scouted to find a way through the next chain of sand dunes.

There were grim reminders out there that not all who attempted this route across the desert were successful. An example was one ill–fated, light blue, four-wheeled rig not yet covered by drifting sand. Painted on the side was "Beep–Beep, the Road Runner" in full stride, depicting the speed and cleverness of the eluder. Back somewhere on a high mountain ridge, shading his eyes, looking south toward the Southern Sahara was Wiley W. Coyote, hungry and contriving to construct an ingenious trap, waiting for the elusive fleet–footed bird to return. "Nevermore" Wiley W. Coyote, that bird is preserved hot and dry in his nest of sand. This Roadrunner, unlike the Phoenix, wasn't about to rise from the sand to be reborn.

No man has ever conquered the sea, conquered a mountain or conquered the desert. He either succeeds or succumbs. The latter joins the silent ones, loved but forgotten through time. Success is held in suspense until the end, as the odds can change with the whim of nature or the adventure traveler's unforgiving blunder.

The odds were changing in this western Niger desert as we had exhausted our reserve of water. As we progressed between the hills of sand there was the relentless glare of the unfiltered rays of the sun and a constant threat of disorientation, or the always pending return of the wind that both make and move sand dunes.

Time passed without conversation other than asking another person for a swallow of water from his canteen. As the hours passed, the sand began to flatten and the mirages became closer and wider. Finally thirty miles of sand dunes were behind us with just a mile or so of level soft sand to negotiate. Sand laddering did not become an art by the skilled. It remained hard work, lifting, pulling and getting lined up with the wheels to be driven over and off again.

After all we had endured, Murphy had to interject his law. Don Murk came over asking, "Where's Ross?" One rider and his bike just weren't with us any more. All of us were together sand laddering in the level sand when a good, reliable rider just disappeared.

53

It seemed the master of the natural deception, a mirage, had done it again, using what may be its oldest trick, that of enticing one of the desert visitors in a game of catch me if you can.

Don and I agreed he couldn't have gone east because of a row of sand dunes to our left with the deposits of deep fall sand made by the westerly winds. Not even an idiot would return to the sand dunes that we had just completed. We swung west and saw no tracks. He had to have ridden on into the mirage, southeast. Looking in that direction, we saw that the sand had ended, leaving a rocky surface where into this mirage we could see a group of phantom motorcycles riding out in the desert. We allowed the others to enjoy the manual art of sand laddering the last few hundred feet, while Don and I rode into the rocky flat land to see if we could locate Ross.

We found no markers, except for an arrow near where we had exited the sand. If there were markers, they would be stacks of stone, and extremely difficult to see. It would be almost impossible to get lined up with these markers.

To bet your life on an old arrow may be foolhardy, but it just seemed the natural way to go. The rock desert is trackless, but out there somewhere was a fort where we could replenish our water supply. We rode slowly, not letting ourselves become part of the game of chase, hoping we would meet our returning buddy.

No such luck. Once the chase had begun, it was difficult to break it off. To stop the chase is to lose and be left alone. To keep on pursuing postpones reality.

The desert mirage doesn't win them all. To our left was the fort, small and nearly covered with sand. I took this opportunity to snap a quick illegal picture before turning from the backside and riding around the front. This may have been the weakest fort, but it was still a military outpost. When we reached the front of the fort, there, soaking in hot sulfur water from an artesian well, was our friend.

This was Fort Assamaka. It must have been the last outpost on earth. The fort was half covered with sand that had drifted through the gate until the gate was rendered useless. The three or four soldiers who came out to fill in the immigration papers merely walked over the walls. These soldier's quarters must resemble a cave, no doubt, without windows or a workable door and, of course, no electricity.

The only things I saw that would be different from the nineteenth century were three poles with wires between, which meant they had radio contact with their commander, who would be in much more pleasant accommodations.

Secondly, the sand had moved. How much, I don't know, but maps were still showing a track on to Agadez. Now that track was high rolling sand dunes. These guys were stuck here. It was two hundred seventy miles or so to their closest town. They would only be able to leave when someone came out after them. As for recreation, they could sit outside at night and curse the darkness, and by day curse the brightness.

By pointing on our map the soldiers informed us there was no way we could continue east toward Agadez. We had to go north two hundred miles without markers and find the markers leading into Arlit. Between this fort and Agadez, the sand dunes had grown to sixty miles wide and four hundred fifty miles long.

This would be a fabulous adventure to cross on dirt bikes. All you would need is an ample amount of gasoline, food, water, a good compass, a responsive throttle and an answered prayer. It was difficult to see such a beautiful, untouched, multitude of sand dunes and turn away without a try.

We washed ourselves in their strong flow well, the first bath since Tamanrasset. Now, with Ross back in our group, we left Fort Assamaka and its soldiers and headed north. This was the same rocky, flat surface from which we had arrived, just another direction. By the time we traveled the two hundred miles north, we would be getting low on gas. It would also be difficult to find the east/west markers as they would be rather small and six miles or more apart, but that would be another day. Soon after leaving the fort, it became dark and we set up camp for the night.

It had been said, " If the duration of one's life is but one night, that lifetime would be well spent if it was spent in the Sahara Desert." This was one of those nights. Lying out beneath that moonless sky, seeing stars that I had never seen before, all was at peace.

After we were settled for the night, Jack Hawthorn charted where we were, using his charts and sextant. As for me, I didn't unpack my tent, just my cot, letting the heavens be my roof. That night I stayed up late to see a constellation so famous that a continent uses its name for a logo. Untold millions of people in Africa hold it in reverence to such an extent that its likeness is reproduced and worn on chains around their necks. Also they wear them as rings and as saddle horns used on the saddles of the desert camels. It is the Southern Cross. The Southern Cross late at night is low and to the right of the Milky Way. As a rainbow promises, did this too hold a silent promise?

There was also a second and ulterior motive for not unpacking that night. No way was I going to leave those virgin sand dunes just lying there unmolested. For the first time ever, those dunes were going to feel the flying touch of my trial universal tires over their rounding backs, soft shoulders and appealing sides.

So it was early in the morning, all alone, riding into dunes that seemed to have no end. I went up and over, bending left and right, riding the ridges and down through their hollows, but never going east without feeling it first. I was shifting through second, third and fourth, then back again, making tight turns, finding a wall of sand to make a hammerhead stall, saving a spill by down shifting and hitting the throttle hard, never riding over my head. At that moment, it was the only world I knew, using the natural forces of nature to keep my bike upright and skimming over the loose skin of this little corner of the world.

Never again will I ever be there, but never will I ever forget making those hammerhead stalls on a wall of sand.

When I was a young man, I bet my date that I could kiss her lips and she wouldn't feel it. A dime was wagered and the attempt was made. I lost and it cost me ten cents. When I returned to camp, I was informed by my buddies that because I rode off by myself which was foolhardy and dangerous, I could do "kitchen police" by myself for the next two nights. Like the kiss that cost me a dime, both experiences were well worth it.

Soon we were on our way, still going north, passing sand dunes on our right. Within a few hours, we never saw the sand dunes again. But then, in all directions was the flat, rocky surface where nothing leaves tracks. We had no markers to go by, just making sure our direction was north, but not too far north.

To the left, we passed and photographed a tree, a good looking, healthy tree six feet tall. There was no other plant life for a hundred miles in any direction. Other than us few men, there was no life of any kind, not even sand fleas or birds; nothing. Except for the two forts, this was the only natural life we had seen in nearly seven hundred miles. Yet this plant stood alone, not clinging to life, but thriving in its realm for it had found life and nutrients without help or guidance. Not being on any track, this tree may never have been seen before or after, but I hope moisture keeps finding its roots, that it can continue to be an example that even in solitude, there is pride and dignity.

That evening, we found our marker for the route taking us into Arlit. That marker meant just one thing. We were going to find our way out of the desert if our gas held out. We made it.

Photo by Sherm Cooper: The soft sand saved the lives of the surprised riders, stopping their bikes within a few feet of a 400 foot drop.

This picture depicts the radiant heat from the sun near the Algerian/Niger border.

The sandstone columns were growing taller from the wind whipping the desert floor deeper as centuries pass.

IX

ONE THOUSAND MILES THROUGH THE SAHEL
19 Degrees North – 7 Degrees East
to 14 Degrees North – 9 Degrees East

I never leave behind what I have learned to know with joy. On her lawn on South Ardmore Street in old L.A., I once bid a final farewell to my grandmother. I still miss her; she was loving and kind. By contrast, the Sahara Desert by day is violent and without mercy, yet tranquil and forgiving by night.

I, too, will forever remember the Sahara and the game of chance we played on her Canadian sized lawn of sand. Akin to spinning the cylinder in Russian Roulette, if you don't hear the click, you lose. In the game of crossing the Sahara, if you don't find the markers, you lose.

For us to lose would be to pass between the markers which were miles apart. In addition, our gas supply was so low that the point of no return had become a growing concern.

However, it wasn't to be, for in the dimness of the light of the third evening after Fort Assamaka, a marker was found. This marker was standing there in silent solitude, easy to miss.

In the early morning light we headed toward the sun, hoping to line up with the old desert caravan route toward Arlet.

An hour had passed when we discovered "Piranha" waiting in hidden silence, looking like innocent basketball sized bushes. The bushes in all of their innocence had captured and held blowing sand. Rather than a meek little bush, they were lethal sandstone hemispheres with a trailing tail. Hit one with your vehicle, it's crash time. Dodging sandstone bushes for two more hours and watching for markers brought us out of the desert and into Arlet where we got our desperately needed gasoline.

Leaving Arlet after replenishing our fuel and water supply, we literally dove deep into the sugar sand of the Sahel. Rather than normal size rounded granules of sand, this was smaller granules of sand dust that had blown in from the Sahara Desert.

This refuse blown in from the largest desert on earth had secured shelter from its mother wind in the thousand mile area extending east and west across the African Continent, creating the belt known as the Sahel. The Sahel is covered with uncounted miles of thorn tree forest grasslands and more barren desert.

Only seven or eight months had passed since their seven-year drought that had been broken by relieving rains. But in that seven years, apparently all grazing livestock and a majority of Tuareg people perished or found shelter adjacent to far off towns.

The first rider to dive into this sea of dust was Tim Rice. With unexpected severity his front wheel was caught by the sea's suction, tossing Tim headfirst into the powdery muck up to his shoulders. After this classic crash, he performed an artful two-arm push up to a height adequate to resume some of his normal functions such as seeing, breathing and tasting.

His helmet and head were a ball of dust with two eyes peering out. After getting his equilibrium established, he started a "spitting fit" to discharge a mouth full of Nigerian gritty topsoil.

Evidence of seven years of relentless drought was ongoing. Outside of Arlet was a city of white pointed tents for refugees from the south. Handfuls of Tuareg people farther south were attempting to retain life in the first grove of trees. Along the trail toward Agadez were circles of stone footings where huts had once stood.

Nearby, elongated low piles of stone were covering the remains of human bodies. But the last to die is never honored with internment. Skeletal remains of camel and cows were not uncommon near the foot tall grass that returned many years too late.

61

On the second day out of Arlet we were riding due east and entered what seemed to be an endless forest of thorn trees, no grass or brush, just an over covering of full-branched thorny trees with a forest of deep soft sand. Within two or three hours, the sand had brought a couple of the riders down time and again. Legs were bleeding from the punishment of falling and not getting clear of the bike when dropped.

Progress was extremely slow and at times ground to a halt while riders picked up a bike off a fallen rider, rubbed the sore spots, rested, then restarted their engines for another try. After a few of those episodes, I left the group, looking for a better way through the forest before we had a major problem with a severe injury.

Sand riding is one-third psychological, one-third skill and one-third internal fortitude to turn on the throttle and let the motorcycle skim on top of the sand where a good bike loves to fly.

My flight over the sand ended quickly. Locking my brakes I bounced to a stop on a built up unfinished roadbed. It seemed unreal that out there in an abandoned wasteland where the only noticeable life was thorn trees, men had endured "bend over" labor, fitting uncountable grapefruit size rounded stones together. This roadbed ended in the trees and sands just a few hundred feet west of where I came to a stop. Looking to the east, the direction we were going, the stone roadbed rose up and over rolling hills in a perfectly straight line as far as could be seen.

If seeing this roadbed deep in the thorn tree forest was surprising, what I saw within the hour upon returning nearly blew my mind.

I was anxious to locate my buddies whom I had left behind earlier in search of a better way out of the forest. In this sea of sand in a world of trees, I knew getting lost could easily happen. But keeping up speed, the bike handling in the loose sandy loam was beautiful but kept me busy dodging trees and following the old trails in reverse.

It was a piece of cake to find my buddies. Because they had to pick up a spilled bike regularly, they left plenty of trails.

After explaining about the road east just two and a half miles south and giving all the help I could, I turned, heading back to the stone roadbed to see where the road led.

In Morocco and in El Salvador when I backtracked, I got into difficult situations. But out here, what could happen?

After hours of plowing and falling in the sand all of us were getting closer to the realization of a firm riding surface to escape this timber of torment.

This was a great experience, shifting into third gear, pulling back on the handlebars, steering with the body and knees, and skimming over the sand. It was not long until I rode into my old path, whipping between the trees. One mile, two miles, and I would break between the trees onto the roadbed. When the roadbed appeared, I rode under the branches, stopping on the narrow surface of the rock road. I was planning on stopping to again survey the area, but what I saw on the other side of the road on its four-foot high bank, were twelve legs.

Looking up from those twelve legs, I was totally astonished. Those were the legs of what appeared to be the tallest camels one could imagine. Draping over their sides were hanging long black robes. Above the robes and concealed within black turbans must have been the faces of three Arabs; no doubt three wealthy, no-nonsense Arab sheiks.

From where they sat in the saddle on tall camels above the four foot high road bank, they had to have been looking nearly straight down on me some ten or twelve feet below. I cannot imagine what they thought seeing a motorcycle rider who was covered with a dusty Belstaff suit wearing a blue helmet with a duck taped duck bill and dark goggles. At least they could see my hands as both were in plain sight still holding onto the handlebars.

I thought I must be in a temporarily bad position for each Arab would have under his robes his clean hand tightly gripping the handle of a long sword.

To add to the excitement, from the canine world a tan, tall, slim dog came running from between the camels' legs, down the bank to check out this biker from the New World's Heartland. The Arabs remained silent and motionless, and the dog, too, never wasted precious throat moisture by barking, but came around the back of my bike to make a smell and taste sample of my left lower leg. I never released my handgrip on either clutch or throttle, but tried to politely nod my duck billed head before leaving.

Carefully feathering out my clutch with a bit of throttle, the last thing I wanted to do was stall my "kick start" bike under the dark hidden Arabic eyes and a half mad dog. I pulled away going east.

Upon leaving I had a constant companion; the tan, tall, slim canine. He put his snout next to my lower left leg. I'm uncertain whether his desires were to chew on my tibia or to dine on my calf. While the mutt was taking his time choosing a flavorful spot to make his insertion, I was negotiating the rocky road.

If this was a bad ride, the worst was yet to come. As I dropped over a hill into a draw, the grapefruit size rocks ended temporarily and in their place were boulders filling the dry wash. Now, I was not certain I could ride down into the boulders and up the other side without crashing, let alone having this galloping flea circus waiting to devour the spoils when I did a headfirst dive into the stone burial ground for the distracted or unskilled.

So I reached into my repertoire of dumb things to do and pulled out the most stupid action possible. I kicked at the dog just before I went in.

That was the last of this canine being Mister Nice Dog. The front part of his face transformed from snout to two jaws full of ivory colored teeth, highlighted by a pair of flesh tearing fangs.

The last thing I was thinking as I dropped down into the boulder dry wash was why did I kick at the dog?

I had to get my weight back to let the front end up and to roll the throttle on to keep the bike straight. The dog was enraged, trying to find a place to penetrate my low boots and Belstaff pant legs. I had to forget the attempted biting and use full concentration to keep the front wheel from kicking out. The bike stayed straight and when the rear wheel dropped in, I gave her full throttle on a straight line up and out. Never looking back, I rode hard until I knolled the highest hill at a safe distance. Then I stopped.

I was remembering the fleet footed, long eared jackrabbits that do not hide in the thickets but stand upright and alert. Not wanting any more surprises from the camel jockeys or their pets, I sat backward on my saddle remaining alert from my high vantage point and reading a paperback book, *Blue Nile* until we were regrouped and moving on.

As the near darkness fell that evening, we saw a smoldering fire consuming a log next to the forest edge with no one around. From the amount of ashes the camp sight appeared to have been used in mid-afternoon. With the builders of the fire gone, we took advantage of this location to spend the night.

In the dimness of evening, I saw a group of people approaching on camels. They stopped and at a distance we looked at each other. Within two or three minutes the dark silhouettes of the camels and drivers changed direction, disappearing, and I felt bad. We had taken their fire and campsite.

The next morning we broke camp before sun up and were moving out, facing the early rising sun. It was two-thirty in the afternoon before we stopped to eat. In those preceding hours we had advanced just forty-four miles but had fixed an unknown number of flat tires.

The Kilmer wrote, "Poems were written by fools like me, but only God can make a tree." In His divine wisdom, trees in arid land were armed with thorns, not only for security and protection but also tasty and fragile leaves. On the negative side, they drop an adequate number of

65

thorns to spear the unexpected, the desperate or marauding intruders.

Thus it was, as intruders we spent quiet hours in the sand on our knees searching for thorns within the tread, loosening axles, pulling off tires, then patching the puncture holes in the tubes left by the needle-sharp thorns.

Since no two trees are alike, the unusual is memorable.

The world is full of unusual communities, but this windblown village in the gently rolling, scorching hot plains, beyond the thorn tree forest, was a small town with houses not more than three-and-a-half-feet tall. These homes were constructed from a yellowish-colored, square, adobe brick. It was not that the residents were unusually small or that they were basement houses. Rather, as sand blows in, the elevation of the land rises until to enter a house a person must descend a sand ramp into the two room dwellings resembling a basement.

There must be a number of forgotten towns to the north that have been covered by the Sahara's relentless movement south. In Guezzam a walled city at the southern tip of Algeria is shown on older maps as being on a trade route with Agdaz, Niger. Now in Guezzam it is cut off by impassable sand dunes to the south and to the east. All that is showing of that city are portions of its black stone walls and square corner of a few roofs.

That afternoon for the first time in weeks, I did not wear my Belstaff suit lowers. Consequently, the prickly burrs from thorny sand burr grass had accumulated in my boots. When we pulled up and stopped by a fender high house, I sat on the roof and changed my socks, giving my sand burr covered socks to a young Arab boy.

They had camel dung roasted chicken for us to buy and eat, but the burnt, nearly black fouls were just not appealing. However, we descended into their living room, which was devoid of furniture, to rest on the cool dirt floor, spending time out of the glaring sun.

Mid–afternoon on the fourth day south of Arlet, we had stopped near an outcropping of rocks to get an indication of where we were in relationship to Agadez and to take a break from hours in the saddle.

It was a week ago that very afternoon we were at Fort Assamaha, deep in the Southern Sahara, where our detour north had begun. At that time we were within one hundred and fifty miles of Agadez and now according to our calculation, after seven days of continuous effort for the past four hundred miles, the elusive town of Agadez was but sixty miles away.

The quiet stocky built Minnesotan, Don Murk, challenged us, "Let's make a run for it." That is all it took, for with one kick starting and full throttle the race to Agadez was on.

From the start it was an old road that had run along a valley's east escarpment, then down into a sand blown broad valley with fork shaped palm trees growing sparsely on either side. I would have loved to photograph such unique trees. I had never seen them anywhere but there. It was my love for a duel in the sand that greatly exceeded my desire to photograph palm trees with double trunks. Thus, I see them only in memory.

The race turned out to be between Sherm Cooper, Don Murk and myself, bending in and around the gradual turns flat out on the two–fifties. The sand surface was smooth and trackless, not even a blemish of any kind since it was smoothed over from the Sahel's last sandstorm. It was a bit nerve–racking at speed while I was in the lead, never knowing what lurked just below the sand surface or what unexpected changes we would encountered in the sand. It is a great sport figuring the fast line through the turns, keeping your aggressive buddies at bay.

After being passed, I became the hound, chasing, crowding, staying out of the soft tracks made by the rider who errors less. The shadows stretched across our route, the valley ended in a higher plain, the surface became firm.

During the last twenty miles we crossed a flat, grassless plain as darkness began to envelop the Sahel. If we had arrived another twenty minutes or so later, we could not have found this desert town in the darkness.

The fourth rider, however, came into town after full darkness, not that he could navigate so well in the dark trackless plains, but it was more probable that he could smell the beer.

Agadez at night was dark with only a few incandescent bulbs dimly lighting but a few places. However, even with the lack of illumination, there was no problem finding the watering hole. We parked our bikes outside the tavern, and as in many places where there are boys, there soon became a crowd curious about our motorcycles and us.

Inside, the tavern had a sandy dirt floor, an L-shaped bar with stools and half a dozen tables with chairs for four. It was a quiet, pleasant saloon with only a few non–Arabic Muslims as patrons, including a young couple in non–Arabic clothing sitting on stools at the bar and another couple at a table nearly out of sight in the dimness of the room.

After relaxing for a while following our wild afternoon ride in from the desert, we walked into the next room where we had been hearing voices and laughter. This room was not unlike the dining room where we had a meal in Tamanrasset a couple of weeks earlier. Four long tables with chairs were set with white tablecloths. There was good lighting and a hard surface floor. The walls were without pictures or decor leaving it dull and drab.

The voices we heard were those of a Swiss crew of six well drillers who had been visiting and singing songs from their native land. One of our riders, I will call him Pete (for obvious reasons), had come in out of the desert using beer's foul smell as his navigational guide.

He must have downed a bottle or two of their high octane, for at the first annoyance from the Europeans' singing, he exploded and jumped up screaming, "Shut up," crazy enough to storm the group single-handed in his violent rage. It took the quick thinking and acting of

Sherm Cooper to get tempers cooled. Sherm was closer to the Swiss, as Pete was on the outside of the tables.

Sherm stood up taking a couple of quick steps over to the sextet, put his hand on a well driller's shoulder, and with the other hand started to lead the group in an all dining room bi-lingual sing-along.

Two more of their crew came and joined the crowd. They were Americans, well drillers from Odessa, Texas.

I engaged in a conversation with the wild one from Odessa. They were trying to go west to Mauritania, but because of thorns and sand, progress had come to a mere few miles each day. The highlight of his tales was a side trip to the island of Madagascar. Telling that was the wildest time ever. He said he spent thirty-six hundred dollars in just a week. No doubt, the next generation of offspring from that locale will be cow ropers who prefer high-heeled leather boots and talking with a Texas twang.

We ate, sang and visited the evening away. Then, getting on our bikes, we backtracked six miles north of Agadez to our camp. Later that night the drunken Pete blasted through camp on his bike with the engine screaming, shaking the tents with sand and sound. Bill Record came out shaking his fist into the darkness, hollering every violent, obscene word in his broad vocabulary.

By daybreak I was up and saw Pete walking into our camp out from the desert sand. Record, too, was up. Seeing Pete walking toward us from out of the sand, Record started swearing, calling him every filthy name from his repertoire of foul thoughts. Between the degrading adjectives he inserted, "Where's my bike?" With this, Pete turned and walked back into the desert, disappearing over a sand dune toward the eastern sunrise.

By chance, a few hours later I met the Odessan well driller who was still half drunk himself. Referring to Pete, he told me, "I wish we had a guy like him in our crew. He rode his motorcycle through the door into the bar, then laid it on its side, burning wheel-spinning donuts."

The Odessan also recounted that after the tables and chairs were straightened, Pete came back a couple of hours later. He rode his bike into the room, raising havoc as before.

Agadez is a nearly forgotten wind swept desert town with apparently no police or law enforcement of any kind. However, at the next city with an airport connecting to the outside world, Pete caught a flight back to the States. Pete's leaving did not compensate for the damage he inflicted to the tavern. If that place was not a non-alcoholic consuming society, the knife-wielding locals may have administered vigilante punishment.

During the morning hours I took a bar of soap and a bucket of water and washed the Algerian dust off my body, then scrubbed my clothes. Being a clean dude, I packed my gear and rode my bike back into Agadez to see the adobe town during the daylight hours.

In town the sandy streets were vacant except for two Arabs leaning against one of the mud brick buildings. The tracks on the sandy streets were footprints and tire tracks left by our motorcycle tires from just a few hours previous.

Virtually every building in town was made of adobe, mostly one story. The Moslem crying-tower, too, is adobe, fifty or sixty feet tall with a few wooden poles protruding out horizontally for structural ruggedness. The crying tower, as well as the lower buildings, was weather beaten and worn to rounded edges from what appeared to have been incessant sand blasting during intensive wind storms.

I left my bike for a walking tour of this antiquated desert town. I walked slowly just to absorb the feeling of what life was like living in old Agadez. The only thing I saw on the street were the two men next to a building. They were fully robed; their faces were unseen. A few moments later an Arabic woman came across the smooth, sandy street to meet me face to face. She was wearing a hooded light-brown robe.

I watched her approaching, her sandaled bare feet gently kicking the course flowing robe. I could see her dark eyes and both of her hands protruding from the robe's folded sleeves. Her arms were crossed in front of her chest holding the loose flowing gown closed.

Without a show of innocence or of being brazen, she pleasantly walked up within inches of me and stopped. With the four fingers of each hand, she opened her robe exposing her upper tan–skinned full body. There, showing it all, was a beautiful young woman possessing an apparent harmless desire to advance her wealth, even within sight of the Moslem crying-tower.

There have been many men whose lives were quickly terminated because they did not have eyes in the back of their heads. I had no desire to join the multitude from a knife of a thief or a jealous suitor, and for sure I did not trust the two faceless men who were standing behind me leaning against the adobe wall. I stepped back while reaching into my leather folder, removed a bill of money and gave it to this young woman.

It was stone quiet on that nameless sandy street. If someone came up behind me I could have heard his footsteps. So I paused for a moment, smiled to this most beautiful young lady, nodded good–bye, and stepping past her continued southward.

I was the only man with a face in sight that morning. Even in the early day's sun, the Arabic men hooded themselves. It was I who was unusual, wearing a clean but dingy shirt and Levis. And to protect my head from the sun I wore a heavily lined, black wool, sun faded Spanish beret. It was not my intention to look different or out of place or to draw attention to myself. However, just two more blocks south on my walking tour of this fresh new day, I was invited into a thick walled adobe home by two more of those dark eyed tan–skinned lovelies. These two were peering out from their doorway. Agadez that morning was an island paradise in a sea of sand.

Now I am not opposed to entering a lady's home to break some bread and drink some freshly brewed tea while relaxing around a dining room table. Ah, but before I lost my money and my health, I reviewed the repertoire of epic dramas including the story of Helen of Troy. It was the colorful and silent spider who beckoned the gullible fly in to dine. Not me! It will take more than flowing black hair, flashing dark eyes with damp sweet lips to entice me into their chamber. Maybe next time.

The author sits in silhouette before the evening campfire.

The weatherbeaten town of Agadez with its prominent
Muslem crying tower.

X

HARBOR FROM THE STORM
13 Degrees North – 8 Degrees East

I was riding near a scrub forest of small bushy trees the day after camping in a Nigerian horse cavalry post on the frontier with Niger. It was a rare day, being rather dark with a low overcast, no wind, just an apparent low-pressure weather change preceding a storm.

I had stopped to answer nature's call and in my modesty walked amongst the tender dry brush for concealment, even though I hadn't seen anything but sandy soil and foliage for hours. Minutes later, a fast moving unseen animal came crashing through the bush. The tinder dry leaf and limbs seemed to be pulverizing in a flash. My emotions went from tranquillity to terror as I jumped forward as it passed behind me. Australia's Crocodile Dundee has his way of handling wild situations, and I have mine. Not waiting to see if "the thing" were being chased by friend, suitors or foe, I circled behind more trees and got out of there.

Some time later the rain commenced. I pulled up, stopping next to a wide heavily foliaged dark green tree. With no indication of lightning activity, I took shelter under that perennial plant as the rain increased to a downpour.

That tree became a natural harbor from the storm, a haven of refuge for all that came. Across to the left was a group of light brown skinned men clad in dusty colored pieces of cloth. None was talking. They just stood in their area to get out of the weather. Then on the right, huddled together, was a pack of wild dogs. They were not the killer dogs of the plains with the sharp rounded ears, but the same sized curs all mingling in a tight group with ears, head and tails down in a subdued behavior.

The broad tree with its thousands of leaves all slanting outward worked in unison keeping this odd and diverse assemblage from becoming soaked. It was I who was faceless and oddest of the group, for I was wearing glasses and a duck billed helmet. Each of us peacefully retained our own territory through the afternoon cloudburst. When the storm subsided, the rain ended. All but I "silently" departed.

XI

A THANK-YOU TO AMERICA
12 Degrees North – 9 Degrees East

Being able to leave Agadez after Pete mangled the furniture in the bar twice the previous night may have been plain good fortune on our part. We certainly didn't know if there was legal law enforcement in that desolate desert town or if vigilantism was administered justice on the spot. Because Agadez is Muslim, aid not be given to a business engaged in selling alcoholic beverages.

During the night or the following day there was no evidence of authority. However, I would not have wanted to be Pete, or mistaken for him if the tavern operator would catch up and attempt to play mumbly peg on his torso with a sharply honed saber.

On the third day south of Agadez, we were spending much of the afternoon in Zinder filling out the usual questionnaires required for being in their city. The paper work was being done under small-leaf shade trees in front of the law enforcement building. I was sitting on the ground in the coolness of the shade when a local teenaged boy came over to visit. During our conversation he told me, "Please thank the people of America for the wheat and other products they sent us during our seven year drought."

This I have done in film and print to show the appreciation that he and the people of the Sahel have for America's compassion of their fellow man.

Kano, Nigeria was the next city south of Zinder. To enter the city from the desert, we had to carefully maneuver through a pair of tank traps set up on the road along a ridge north of the city.

The tank traps were each made of three heavy, twenty-five-foot, steel pipes welded as a two-foot horizontal triangle. Numerous steel barbs, strong enough to penetrate anything that tried to breach them, extended at angles upward from the main frame. They were set to stop virtually any vehicle coming in from the desert or leaving the city except at a very low speed. To maneuver through, a vehicle had to stop and turn forty-five degrees with little room to spare to prevent anchored barbs from penetrating a vehicle's belly, wheels or tracks.

Kano was a rather large, somewhat busy melting pot of race and culture where Chinese and Indian businesses were well represented.

After cleaning up following the five-day ride in from Agadez, I stopped in a shoeshine parlor to have my boots saddle soaped and polished.

The operator was a shiny, black-skinned man who had artistically cut tribal markings on both sides of his face. He told me they identified his tribe and also his father's identity. He continued by revealing his inability to secure employment because of his facial carvings.

Two local Englishmen were amazed that he had come in from the desert and even more so that he had crossed from the Mediterranean.

There are always street girls, but what really turned my head were the light skinned men pedaling bicycles through the streets with live chickens, in coops, balanced on their heads.

XII

A DAY FOR A PARADE
7 Degrees North - 14 Degrees East

We came into the city of Ngaoundere, Cameroon, after spending Christmas Eve camped near the Nina River between two native villages. To give a Christmas atmosphere to our campsite, we bound some tall elephant grass together near the tassels, creating our version of a Christmas tree. For decoration, we wrapped toilet tissue around a few times, ending near the tassel. With the flickering yellow campfire light dancing on the white tissue, it became rather colorful, but without our loving families it wasn't fulfilling.

Two of our fellows left to spend a portion of Christmas Eve in the nearest village. Because of the loud instrumental music via the bongo drums serenading all within hearing distance, we knew where the action was.

As a compatible gesture, the local farmer, in whose dry cornfield we were parked, brought over a jug of hooch, early day slang for liquor. The junior member of our group drank some and temporarily attempted to act drunk.

Christmas Day in Ngaoundere, Cameroon, was a day for a parade. Just by chance I was in the right place at the right time. For, without a sound except for the clippity–clop of walking horses, here came a parade.

These were not the average horses clippity–clopping, but the finest, for each large sorrel was well groomed and had brushed shining hair reflecting crescent shaped glows from the equatorial sun's morning rays. Mounted were the area's territorial chiefs. Most wore flowing colorful garments, sitting tall with an austere,

78

no–nonsense manner in the saddle. They, too, carried long spears, but in a more aggressive slant than their serfs. Each horse had adornments of precious metals, colored leather and cloth.

Escorting their chiefs were anywhere from ten to twenty personal serfs or slaves of each chief's jurisdiction. The escorts were more like a small personal military guard, each man keeping a rigorously self–disciplined manner. They protected their chief, or gave the appearance of protection, as they walked in front of and on both sides of him, carrying long spears in a vertical position.

Seeing the spectacle of personal power in a colorful parading column nearing me, I realized I stuck out like Malcom X at a Ku Klux Klan convention. I was their only spectator. No one was on the street. Even my buddies had found a place to relax behind a swinging door. Looking for some semblance of security, I stepped behind a slim utility pole, watching and photographing.

As the parade passed, it was impressive to view the items, materialistic and characteristic, that gave the chiefs the appearance of superiority. One of the high sitting chiefs had the semblance of being hard–boiled and mean. Rather than attired in ceremonial splendor, he carried the weight of full body armor. It was not like the armor of Medieval European soldiers, but a close mesh, fully flexible and shiny body, arm and upper leg protection. The suit was made of thousands of small, movable metal pieces fitted together in such a way as afforded protection from hand propelled weapons and yet did not diminish his movements.

This chief's face and body language were that of a contemptible, treacherous, violent human being. When he saw me watching and photographing him, he turned his horse toward me, raising his spear in a threatening gesture.

Rather than cow–towing to that iron clad bully, I stood facing him and took his picture. He came nearly in range to jab me. I did not retreat because I feel all men are basically good. (I have been wrong before.) No doubt, a well-placed spear could be used to sharply adjust my foolish attitude.

Where I have come from, have heard of or have been, we all love a parade. In Ngaoundere, Cameroon, it appeared to be only I who loved the parade. It has never been difficult for me to adjust to the customs of another land, but not to photograph a parade is like not picking up a fork when a plate of food is served. It is like not twisting a throttle while sitting on a motorcycle. There are certain things that just go together.

In America, if a person can read, there is no need to know anything. We have warning labels such as, "Do not smoke the cigarette;" "Do not forget to take your pill;" "Do not get into the refrigerator to see if the light goes out." If they had had the American government, there would have been a warning label of adequate size and legibility at a stated distance, which read, "Do not photograph the chief. It could be hazardous to your health."

Before our midmorning's departure from Ngoundere, I spent some time visiting with a Catholic nun. She and a second person were in a car on the street, the only automobile I had seen in days. She not only was a vibrant and interesting conversationalist, but she wore a pair of gold lace earrings. They looked as if they were made by tatting fine gold thread, creating a truly unique design. Earrings similar to hers would have been a beautiful gift for my dark-eyed wife, who never objects to my sojourns from far–away places.

Departing southward, the road we followed gained altitude for miles until we were in the Cameroon Highlands. This Christmas day was being celebrated in the villages with gaiety, music and dancing. The men in their finest apparel were in long white cotton robes. The women's finery was cotton print in blue, red, green, brown and black with each wearing a wrap–around head scarf from the same material as their dress. Everyone in the villages seemed happy, and they appeared to be a very caring people. I stopped and joined their festivities of music and dancing, taking a photo or two.

As we rode on through the highlands there was a cut into the side hill leaving an eight-foot-high bank on the right hand side of the dirt road. Either some wild Brahmas were feeling their oats or were spooked. Whatever the cause, the effect was the same. A small herd stampeded off the high road bank. When they came flying past, Dave Ray collided with one in mid air. He hit the cow with enough impact to change its projectory, causing it to land on her side, all four legs nearly upward.

The heifer floundered for a moment, attempting to find what direction was up. Finally getting her hooves to dig dirt, she righted herself, looked back, then scurried down the hill through the trees.

Dave did quite well considering his adversary. He only suffered from badly cut fingers and a sore knee.

While we were getting Dave road-worthy again, a baboon came wandering around looking us over, butt up and eyes toward us.

When a baboon moons you and it looks you in the eye shaking its head, it gives you the impression that baboons may not hold us superior primates in their highest esteem.

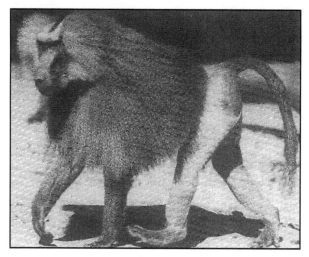

When you're mooned by a baboon, it gives the impression that baboons may not hold us superior primates in their highest esteem.

After I took the chief's picture, he turned his horse toward me, raising his spear in a threatening gesture.

XIII

A RUSSIAN MILITARY CIRCUS
4 Degrees North – 18 Degrees East

Thursday morning, December 26, we left the nation of Cameroon. In doing so we were leaving some of the happiest people we had seen.

The crossing into the Republic of Central Africa was more than forty miles southeast of Meiganga, Cameroon. The buildings at the frontier were weather- bleached, wooden structures that once stored farm grains.

Sitting in the shade to protect themselves from the equatorial sun and leaning against one of the buildings were two men, each desiring to hitch a ride. The first was a New Zealander named Paul. The second was a young Oriental from Japan.

This Asian fellow joined us until we reached the first town in RCA. There he left us possibly to walk back to Cameroon. If Paul insisted on waiting for a ride, he might as well have taken up residence where he was. RCA is the size of a Midwestern state. In the trek across, we did not see any four-wheeled vehicle or even a tire track.

The road to Bovar, the first town in the Republic of Central Africa, was exceptionally rough. Grass had overgrown the surface and bridges were non–existent. However, between washouts and water crossing, the track was footpath smooth.

Farther on there was a region of low mountains with long board valleys. There the sky had become totally overcast with a stagnant haze caused by local farmers setting fires trying to keep small plots of land cleared of

83

vines so they could graze cows and possibly rid the area of Titus flies.

In one of the jungle villages I stopped to watch a native woman torch her own hut. Obviously her dwelling was infested beyond a harmonious co-existence. As the flames leaped high above the scorching hot, rounded thatched dwelling, good sized birds dove through the flames, attempting to snatch a hot meal from the bounding bugs jumping out to their sure demise.

The road going on was the usual grassy, sandy loam with an occasional water crossing. The French, their industries and their vehicles had departed this Equatorial African nation a few years earlier. As we crossed their country, the only visible industry we saw was a few head of Brahma.

On the track leading up into the nearly deserted town of Babor, going was so difficult that it became necessary to down shift, then work our way through deep washouts. Gully washers had turned ruts into miniature ravines with protruding boulders. Babor's business district was a wide dirt street a block long with oil stained buildings on each side. Two businesses were open. One was a bar with very welcomed boiled eggs sitting out in a glass dish.

There were two more days of jungle trails before reaching the town of Bouali. That road was a continuation with the same conditions except for the surface. It turned from a sandy loam to red volcanic lava. The volcanic lava was so fine it penetrated into our pores, clothing and into our equipment. The riding conditions, however, were fabulous. The bike continued to handle perfectly in the rose-red dust and was a joy to ride.

Again the jungle ended and taking its place was a yellow, hard clay hill that was cut to ribbons by erosion. Over the crest was the nearly abandoned town of Bouali.

It was unique. The jungle side of the nearly vacated community appeared to be adandoned: a bare street with dilapidated and neglected small, yellow clay adobe homes. However, on Bouali's east-end where traffic may have come in from the capital city of Bangui, there was a roadside stand. It was nothing big, about the size of a motorcycle shipping crate, yet a private enterprise was trying to flourish. The business was the buying and selling of bottled beverages. In addition, the proprietor was offering a one–of–a–kind on the retail market, Milk Shakes Direct. The milk shakes were local cows' milk with Ovaltine. There, sitting on the proprietor's wooden bar was the dark jar of chocolate malt flavored Ovaltine with its traditional orange label.

The milk container must have been the brown cow tethered next to the stand that, in modern terminology, produced on demand. No one ordered a milk shake, but I could speculate as to the formula. Four tablespoons of Ovaltine and a few gentle squeezes of the udder's spigots into a glass, and presto, a warm, mild shake.

It always takes a biker a couple of minutes to pull off his helmet and hang his gear on the handlebars. By that time six of the brightly dressed gals from the east-end of Bouali were making themselves available. None were crude like some of the young stateside prostitutes. These young women were more like ladies who knew how to present themselves, whether they were just looking at something interesting and unusual or were offering the desired commodity for sale.

I never asked to find the answer. However, one of the women I remember with the highest respect and esteem. As I walked up, this full-breasted woman was nursing a baby; she turned looking at me. I, no doubt, was an unusual sight for her as I got off my motorcycle. I was dusty, unwashed, and the last time I bathed I was a white guy.

On the other hand, she was just as proud and graceful as the others. What made her more notable was that she had only two–thirds of her face remaining, for she had been afflicted with leprosy; the other third of her face was healed over. There was no way for me to know if young people in her town teased and ridiculed those who are different or if she was strong and rose above the torment of others if they did.

The sextet may have been an impromptu, unofficial welcoming committee. If that were their intention, they were totally successful. They looked good in their dress of wrap-around cotton print (from a bolt) with matching cloth head coverings, resembling a donut twist. They retained a bashful serenity.

Do you suppose we had been pounding the saddles too long, and anything in a skirt brought a second look? Or were the girls looking for an evening of song and samba to the rhythm of jungle music? We never found out, but the bottom line was, each of us enjoyed seeing with whom we shared the streets of Bouali.

Just before we left, a young American, whose name I understood to be Vos Semble, rode up on his Honda 90 motorcycle and stopped to visit. He looked to be in his late teens.

His Honda was the only motor vehicle in Bouali and the first vehicle of any type we had seen for a number of days, going back to Central Cameroon. And he was only the third non–Negroid that we had seen since Kano, Nigeria. The other two were the New Zealander named Paul, and the oriental from Japan. They were both at the border crossing leaving Cameroon. As I mentioned earlier, the Japanese had joined us for awhile, but left us at the first village in RCA, saying he would rather stay with the natives.

The young American, who seemed to be living alone, was helping to develop fishponds for food. He told us that the sixty–two-mile, gravel road into the capital city of Bangui, which was never maintained, was so rough that it was a two-hour drive. How correct he was. If you could take the incline of each bump, pothole and ripple, stack them into a giant incline, it would make a mountain thirty miles high. As Vos cautioned us, it was a bumpy road.

The sixty-two-mile drive lacked the beauty of the jungle. Much of the jungle area had been burned. Rather than vines and trees, there were old dead horseweeds. Our replacement riders, who flew into Bangui airport later that night, told us of large numbers of jungle fires which could be seen burning during the flight.

After arriving at the entrance of Bangui, it took two or three hours of filling out papers and answering questions before being admitted through the city gates.

With a totalitarian government in addition to the Soviet Union's military presence, those birds at the city gates wanted to know everything from my hat size to my tire pressure. In the heat of the afternoon, we were told we could be on our way.

Going south and east, but continuing on the north side of the city, we arrived at a mission where we would be staying. Just as soon as I stashed my gear and washed the accumulation of dust and grit down the drain, I left for the American Consulate in the main part of the city. Surprises never end. We had only been in Bangui a couple of hour and, incidentally, just on the north side of town. The Consulate already knew we were in the city.

Apparently after forty five hundred miles in the saddle with six weeks of adventure, I had lost my ability to just sit down and visit. Or was it that I had no desire to relate experiences, even with an American, while still on the cone shaped continent?

The Consulate was a perfect place to leave my bike while spending the remainder of the afternoon walking the streets to see what I could have been missing by living in our country's heartland. I left the consulate on foot for a walk near the Ubangi River and through the markets.

Bangui, as a capital, wasn't large or busy. There were mostly one-story buildings along hard surface streets. And that day, at least, the market near the river was nearly deserted. But the entertainment was international, for coming down the street, in close proximity to the market and river, was a column of three Russian military amphibious tanks.

Now, I'm a motorcyclist, not a military observer. But this is my interpretation of this Russian military exercise as I saw it from my sidewalk vantagepoint.

The driver of the lead tank must have been a veteran of the sixties rock music era, and the only thing he could hear was the ringing in his ears. On their army tanks, the antennae whips sprang perfectly, no problems there. However, from what I had observed of Russian electronics at the World's Fair in Montreal that my daughter Kathy and I attended in '67, if you couldn't decipher static, you couldn't enjoy Russian Radio.

Thus, the old and reliable form of transmission of command was used between tanks – SCREAMING!!! The commander of the column was on the second tank. I wasn't close enough to read his nametag, but I thought I recognized him as the head clown with the Barnum and Bailey Circus and using the name, Commander Tuffshitski.

With no hope for the reception between radios to be overheard above static and clank of the tanks, the "rock" deaf driver in tank number one was unable to differentiate between screaming and ears ringing. Commander Tuffshitskie, wearing a floppy eared helmet, prepared to make direct contact with the lead driver by jumping from his number two tank to the number one tank. That's when the "rock" deaf one saw the desperate reflection in the mirror of "Floppy" preparing to jump. Trying to lip-read a scream in the mirror, he hit the brakes to get a closer look. He apparently was still a novice at lip reading. The brakes are the only thing I can report that worked perfectly, as number two tank slammed into the stopped number one tank, sending the commander, still wearing his floppy eared helmet, flying head first over the turret of number one tank, where he grabbed on as tank number three hammered number two tank like a twenty ton croquet mallet. That, in turn, bashed number two tank into number one again. The commander, still wearing his floppy eared helmet, was gripping and hugging the turret like a rock climber who had just lost his foothold, not wanting to be the first "Russian Tortilla" to be rolled out flat on the streets of Bangui.

Above my laughter as I kept walking, not looking back, I could hear the Russian tenor in tank number three shouting, "Tuffshitskie, Tuffshitskie!"

That's how it was on the afternoon of December 28, 1974, in the streets of Bangui. Only the names were added for clarification.

That evening was going to be the last evening with a few of the riders, some of whom I would never see again. Replacement riders were coming in during the wee hours of the night on a flight arriving from Europe.

A good sit-down meal was in order, so all of us walked together to a taxi cab driver and asked if he would take us to a restaurant. We were all able to get in his taxi the normal way except for Barnie Coski. He climbed into the trunk with his feet sticking out. Before arriving at the cafe, a policeman stopped us. He was really angry. Angry was the conservative description of this cop's emotions.

Unable to understand his dialect, we surmised he had remembered watching American news reports of voter registration days down in the South and thought we were taking a Southern agitator to an Alabama landfill to be planted. And he didn't approve of Southern justice.

It was a sensitive situation. But it was settled that the taxi was too full and Barnie had to run alongside holding onto a door handle until we arrived at the cafe. Tall, wiry Barnie didn't mind and made it in full stride.

The cafe could be described as a thatch–roof shelter held up by wooden poles. But it had something we were really looking forward to, table and chairs. It took a while to get used to leaning back while sitting down. We had only used chairs twice in the last month and a half. That was in Agadez and Tamanrasset.

When a waiter came over, we let him know we would like anything he brought us as long as he brought us real meat. That he did. It was Zebra liver and steaks. He brought each of us two pieces of meat, a mashed vegetable and a small footbal-shaped loaf of bread, all served on a round plate. A meal should be a memorable occasion, and this one was. Food and fellowship were never to be forgotten.

In all our times together, we never really visited. Not once did anyone mention the perils of the Southern

Sahara or the deep, endless sugar dust of the Sahel. Rather, we had good times of laughter and joking.

In the forty five hundred miles behind us, the logical ones had quit. The reckless and foolish kept refueling and shifting gears and, in my opinion, are better men because of it.

It's hard to believe. But, on returning to the mission where we were going to stay, I washed again. That's twice in one day. Back in the desert, it was twice in one month, whether I needed to wash or not.

Getting ready for bed, I went over to my bunk that was made-up with both white sheets and a pillow. That's where I stopped. There was no way I could open the white mosquito net curtains and lie down. It just didn't seem the thing to do. So, turning around, I picked up my tent and sleeping roll and walked out amongst the trees. I camped for the night near where my bike was parked. Sherm must have shared a similar feeling, for his tent was already up.

Pygmies observe a quiet day in their village deep in the Congo jungle.

XIV

ON FOOT IN THE CONGO JUNGLE
2 Degrees North – 18 Degrees East

By morning light I was up, had stashed my gear, and returned to the mission's dorm to see the replacement riders who flew in during the night. Looking through the mosquito netting over the bed, I saw a guy I once knew. I shook his shoulder saying, "Hey, Bettencourt, how did you leave things in Massachusetts?"

"Jerry, you old flat tracker," he replied. "I haven't seen you since the road race at Wilmont Hills" (Wisconsin).

One fellow was enough to awaken. There would be six weeks to get acquainted with the rest, so I left for the post office to see if a letter from my wife Jo and baby daughter Belinda was waiting in their General Delivery. I knew we were going to be held up from crossing the Ubangi River into Zaire for a day or two. Therefore, with an early start possible, I could find a way for some good exploring along the river.

It was still early when I arrived at the river dock. Mingling around a good-sized boat were five people that looked as though they were ready to travel. Walking over, I started visiting with an American from the desert country of Chad, in Central Africa. They were taking a trip down river to the Republic of Congo.

I said, "Hey, hold the boat. I'll get my buddy and join you."

Sherm Cooper was going into the post office just as I was leaving only a few minutes earlier. Remembering this, I started my motorcycle and sped down Bangui's empty, early–morning streets to catch him. Thankfully, Sherm's Honda was still leaning on its side stand in front of the postal building. I parked my bike, ran up the steps and met him just as he was ready to leave. I told Sherm about the river trip. His only reply was, "I have a filthy shirt on. We'll wash it on the boat."

What good fortune this was, traveling all day down one of the ten major rivers of the world through an area where there have been possible sightings of huge river serpents or dinosaurs. And then we had the opportunity the next day to explore in the jungles of the Congo.

River travel is fabulous, not as fast moving or adventurous as the motorcycle trails, but enjoying a totally different view. The jungles came to the water's edge. There were clearings along the banks every few hours where native villages, similar in appearance and hut construction to the locations of the ones along the Rio Grande in Jamaica, appeared. With this being the dry season, the river level was low. So, a boatman hanging over the bow, kept measuring the river depth by using a line with markers, then calling the reading. It was the same activity that gave Samuel Clemens the pen name Mark Twain.

Up ahead a new dugout canoe, unstained and still its cream colored natural hue, came out into the channel near the course of our boat. A line was thrown, and one of the two natives caught the line and pulled the dugout speeding alongside. We did not slow down. From inside the canoe, a pig, maybe a twenty-five pounder with its four feet tied, was thrown onto the deck of our boat along with a stock of ripe bananas. In return they tossed down a bottle of what was once called in the Midwest, Southern Comfort. As it went over the side, I didn't see a label. It must have been that famous home brew.

As the day passed, the evening shadows darkened the shore lines. Even with a near full moon over the silver waters, it became difficult to distinguish the water's edge.

Around a turn on the river's right bank was a bonfire casting its yellow reflection across the wide waters of the Ubangi. The engine was idled back and the reflections began to shorten as we neared a village. The engine was shut down. We drifted close to a small river pier just out from the bonfire that had been our guiding light. We bumped the bow in first. It was secured. In the nearly currentless water the stern was pulled taut and it, too, was made fast.

This would be my first night without sleeping next to my bike. For the past six weeks my bike had been my only conveyance. Now my conveyance would be my gray sneakers. The fire's glow revealed village huts; to the left lay a hard grassless gray clearing. Beyond the trees, to the right, another fire disclosed a larger community away from the river's flood plain.

It wasn't long before a good-sized crowd had gathered and dancing commenced. Like anywhere else I've been, these people, too, were good to be around, fun loving and seemingly kind. They wanted us to be part of them. As the men came over extending their hands, they grabbed our wrists to dance to their music. To this rhythmic samba we would shuffle to the left and shuffle to the right in small circles.

It may have been that in a pleasant evening's harmony we melded into a social compatibility. Or it might have been that music is a catalyst, binding friendships. Whatever the reason, we were among friends on this river's edge.

Before long we left the dancing and walked around the village before hitting the bunks for a restful night's sleep, still to the rhythm of their jungle music. We never realized the reward we would receive the following day.

By daylight, the three of us Sherm, the American from Chad and I, were up and ready for a six-hour walk into the jungles.

We ate what was offered on the boat and took a little more for our trek into the domain of the Pygmies. We knew the Pygmies hid their villages so skillfully that even the regular natives could not find the locations. But we were there and had the time, so we gave it our best shot.

The first village we came to was on a well-beaten path. The soil was hard, yellow clay on which it was easy for the villagers to build their round huts. But these people were like another sub race, much different from the regular natives living along the river. Their skin was lighter in color. Their faces were shaped differently, longer and less round, and they noticeably enjoyed the love and closeness of their children.

The trail beyond was gray, dry dirt or leaf-covered, always smooth but so narrow it would have been difficult to follow by outsiders except during daylight. The deeper into the jungle we walked, the more crooked and less used the trail became. Twice we met two Pygmy men. The American with us tried to communicate to them that we would like to visit their village. Both times the Pygmies passed us by.

Occasionally when there was a break in the overhead foliage, I could see a palm tree rising above the jungle. By looking carefully at the palms, I could see they were tapped, and thus I knew there was a village within walking distance. The Pygmies I had seen earlier were healthy, giving me an indication that they did not drink from water holes. But rather, they tapped the palm juice by inserting a small bamboo tube into the trunk of the tree just under or at the place the palm leaves splayed out near the tree's top. Then using a vine as a cord, the Pygmies tied a gourd to catch the sap, which secreted from the palm tree's wound.

It seemed to us we had seen the last Pygmies we were going to meet as time and distance passed. In the hours of walking we had met just two pairs of the little people. At last we again met more. This time there were three Pygmy men and as before, the American spoke to them. However, rather than passing us, they turned around and ran away. We had no idea what that meant, but one thing was sure, at least they knew we were coming.

The foliage was so dense, one could see no more than a foot and a half to either side as we had to continue walking in single file.

The narrowness of the path restricted our view of the beauty of the jungle. However, the bright shining rays of the sun were seen where the huge jungle trees had forced their way up through the ever-heavy clinging vines.

Walking in sneakers on the soft soil and talking with a low tone in this near tunnel of leaves, we never challenged a monkey colony, insects or birds.

It was so peacefully inviting, I was reminded of a line from a child's poem, "...come into my chamber, said the spider to the fly." Supposedly the fly had no anxiety of continuing . Neither did we. However, because of the expression on the faces of the three Pygmy men when they turned and ran from us, there was some concern.

We knew the Pygmy villages were hidden deep in the jungles away from the trails that are shared by both man and beast. If it were not for the remoteness of their villages and cleverly hidden homes, these small, nearly defenseless people would not have survived through the centuries.

I was leading as the other two behind me were talking. That's when I saw the three Pygmy men again. This time the first one was facing to the right side of the trail with his hands down together, palms up, motioning me to lift the vine. This I did. Before me was a tree trunk lying crosswise with scratch marks showing it had been crossed repeatedly; however, at the vine where I turned in, there was no indication that a cross trail existed.

I handed the vine I was holding to the person behind me while entering the smallest, lowest trail I had ever traveled. If a person like myself, even in the daylight, would make an error by hurrying, he could become hopelessly lost within ten feet, never to find his way again. I kept losing the trail. Then, a pattern set up, at least on this path. There was a big jungle tree every few hundred feet and always on the right hand side. At times we had to climb over the trunk of a fallen tree by using both hands and feet, while also bending under low vines since the Pygmies never used a knife to make this trail.

If there were any danger, I wasn't aware of it. For without thought, I completely trusted the men who showed us into their little corner of the world where a full-sized person may never have entered before. My anticipation was overwhelming as I stepped over a log and turned to the right around the trunk of a massive tree into a peaceful little village located a long, long way from anywhere.

As we entered their village, we just stood and looked at each other. The community was about the size of a rounded basketball court providing area for six, half-walnut shaped huts about the size of a round Volkswagen Bug.

I don't know what they saw in the three of us. But I saw a group of peaceful, caring people who had been living, except for one knife they had acquired, like this for thousands of years.

I had had only two or three minutes back in Bangui to buy gifts to bring with me on this impromptu side trip, so I had purchased coins which I gave out to each person from youngster to adult. The coins seemed to please them. However, they have no place to keep anything and nothing to keep.

There were two details I observed that confirmed what I had seen on the jungle trail earlier. The Pygmies wore waistbands made of fern palm leaves to help them climb the tall palm trees. They also had a few gourds. I did not look to see what was in them, but the gourds were like the ones used for collecting palm juice from the trees back on the main trail.

There was a small fire smoldering near one of the huts. It would have been interesting to see how they started the fire. With no lights, nor any musical instruments and nearly twelve hours of equator jungle darkness, I do not think this would be conducive to happiness. Only they know the answer. Possibly after the hunt, there are long exciting stories to tell and ancestors to remember.

There aren't many groups of people who can enrich one's life just by meeting them. But the four and one-half foot tall people who live deep in the jungle and have nothing but each other are one of them. I hope that each of us has fond memories of each other and that these nearly defenseless people may remain hidden for thousands of years more.

Most communities of human inhabitants are hundreds of years in age. In contrast, the duration of a Pygmy village is measured in weeks. When nearby hunting is nearly depleted, and living conditions complicated by the lack of toilet facilities and the intrusion of insects into their huts, they merely walk away to a fresh area in the jungle and build another tiny town.

In every meeting there is a time for leaving. The time to leave these small people and their cluster of little huts had arrived. I thought I would have enjoyed staying with them, going on hunts, living off of game that was taken using only a blowgun and poison arrows. However, with my luck at hunting, I would have been dining on grubs dug from under dead tree bark and sitting out rainstorms soaked to the skin. Believe me, it was just a passing thought.

We bid good–bye with true sincerity to these people we share our planet with and left as we came, in single file past the huge tree at the village edge and turning left.

It was going to take a bit of masterful jungle navigation to find our way out. First of all, at their village tree, trails went in all directions. It was critical to get started correctly and not err, or we would become hopelessly lost. Most of the narrow low path could not be identified as a path except by looking forward into the leaf–lined tunnel.

We were on our own. The three Pygmy men who showed us the entrance to the path did not come to the village with us. They may have followed and hidden or have gone on, this not even being their village. Whatever the case, we never saw them again.

Exiting the rain forest I knew would not be easy. Twice in my life I have become lost. Once in Michigan, even as I was watching, the world turned around. Not only did the world turn, but it also concealed my tracks, preventing me from following my own tracks back out. (Never will I let this happen again if I can prevent it.)

The little tunnel through the vines was straight ahead. It could have been any direction, but it seemed to be due east. Under an equatorial sun, who knows. If it had rained while we were in there, the leaves would have opened wide. Occasionally there was an opening to the right causing us to make a decision. We all remembered that the trail in was rather straight and the big trees, as we departed, should always be to our left.

At times there were no vines, letting us walk upright, but soon again we had to crouch to get under more of those creeping plants.

As we had come in earlier, there were three of the huge jungle trees on the right hand side of the trail so close to the trail we had to step over their high exposed tree roots. We finally came upon the first tree with the high roots on our left, good evidence we were indeed on our trail out. It was imperative not to become complacent but to keep our own trail in line and not get caught "Y"ing off where the path was indefinite.

We came upon the second, then the third huge jungle tree. At the third tree there was a slight clearing without a defined path beyond. Going back beyond the tree and sighting across the clearing, again we could see where the path should be, as we were sure at this point there was no turn. Going forward not more than five or ten minutes on a very unclear path, we came to a stop.

This was the end of the Pygmy trail. We were nearly positive of this because of a log crosswise and a curtain of heavy foliage just beyond the fallen tree. There was no place else to go. Comments such as, "This has to be it," and "Let's find out," were made in uncertain anticipation. I reached down next to the log's bark running my hand through the leaves until I found the vine's main runner. I started to lift with one hand, then both, until I could see beneath and beyond the vine I was holding. All I saw was a solid wall of more leaves.

At first my stomach tightened as I was thinking that we were in major trouble, lost. We were all speechless as we bent low, passing under the vine and over the log. The next wall of vines was just a hand's reach away, but in between there were green leaves on the ground. Glancing left and right, we hoped this was our trail to start our return trek out.

We carefully pushed the vine into its natural hanging position to again hide the entrance to the Pygmy village.

We knew we were a long way from the Ubangi and the River Queen and had no guarantee we could still find our way back. If the boat operator lost his patience and left without us, our life style would change overnight to the natural way of life. We would see how hospitable the natives really are on one of their bad days.

Standing upright for the first time since leaving our latest acquaintances, we left for the river. It seemed north, but we agreed that was impossible. Since we had left the boat on the starboard side while still facing down stream (toward the South Atlantic) we had to be on the north side of the Ubangi heading in a southerly direction. We knew we turned right into the little path and left when we came out.

There was no danger now of being lost, but the male ego must always know his directions and be in command of the situation. The bottom line was we knew we wouldn't be in command of anything if we arrived back too late at the river village and the boat had already departed for Bangui.

Long ago we had eaten what we brought with us. It was not only the fear of being left, but also hunger that quickened our steps. We still wondered why the jungle was so quiet. Of all the hours in this jungle, the only sounds heard were those we made.

Even the Pygmies said nothing. We didn't mind that we never flushed a bird that would alert the animal kingdom. More than anything, we didn't have any desire to come face to face with a big four-footed feline or round-faced furry primate that might have misunderstood our intentions.

The trail bent back and forth, and as we rounded bends on this trail we met nothing, not a hanging snake, a crawling insect, nothing but leaves and occasional gray tree trunks that protruded with the great heights of their limbs above the jungle roof.

Although the river was a considerable distance away, we continued walking in the eerie silence of the jungle. Two years before this experience I had been held in detention because of a traffic accident in the Grenada prison in Nicaragua, Central America. It, too, had an eerie silence. The commandant of the prison was called "the coroner." There may be a similarity between daytime in the jungle and life in that prison. Make a noise and you are dead. Who knows?

There were reasons not to hurry. First of all, we were not certain this was our trail out, and we wanted to see a recognizable tree to be positive. Second, as we came in there were Pygmies on the trail giving us a sense of security. Jungle trails always take the path of least resistance winding their ways through. Consequently, we were constantly going around trees and heavy vine growth on a narrow footpath worn grassless by feet larger and more numerous than those of our darker cousins.

Segregation is unheard of in the rain forest of Equatorial Africa. The wild beast of the jungle and the homosapien must use the same footpath by timely avoidance.

At last I saw the palm tree that had escaped suffocation from the crawling, clinging vines and had grown high above the green cover of the jungle. I walked beyond, then stopped and looked up from the other side. This was the same tree that I had seen just a few hours earlier, tapped, with a gourd hung to catch its juices.

Not one living thing broke the apparent code of silence as we walked quietly Indian-style through the arched, covered trail. If this were the tall timber of the Midwest, the blue jays would be screeching like the squeak of an old rusty cistern pump. Or we would be hearing the large black crows that pride themselves as "sentries of the forest" cawing, while circling high above, to alert all breathing things of an intruder in their domain. The last thing we wanted was to surprise a beast head on and become his tasty morsel or to be trampled into earthly nutrients.

We stopped for a break under an overhead clearing where the sun broke through the jungle foliage.

Reminiscing on how fortunate we were to have been shown this Pygmy village and to have been able to stay on the right track to get out was the nourishment we needed for another couple hours of walking before reaching the river.

If I were put on a witness stand, I would have to swear on oath I saw or heard no evidence of life other than Pygmies and plants. The Pygmy's primary diet is from living things. They would have to hunt by day and be equally silent. With their small slim bodies and two-foot long bows, they can slip through the vines of the jungle. To become disoriented and lost is human. Life for them must be harsh.

Moving on as before, we saw nothing but leaves and the bark of an occasional tree. The trail ended as we came into the village where the unique native people lived. This time no one was in sight. In the hours spent after leaving the Pygmy village we did not see one living thing.

Our concern heightened again with the thought of being gone too long. I really did not cherish the thought of us three guys becoming white natives of the Congo and learning to Samba. The other alternative would be to find and con somebody out of a dug-out canoe and paddle one of those heavy monstrosities up river for two hundred miles, eating, sleeping on, and drinking who knows what.

It was another half-hour of hiking along this broad trail before we reached the riverside village. There, tied up as we left her, was the boat that we referred to as the "River Queen." She had brought us down river from Bangui the previous day and was waiting patiently for us to return for the upriver voyage to Bangui. Eureka!

The people in charge of this vessel must have been unusually thoughtful, for back on the dock in Bangui the previous day when I was told of their plans to travel down river to the Republic of the Congo, I did not ask, just hollered, "Hey, wait for me."

Now on the return, only they knew how many hours we were delayed, for when we came out of the

101

jungle without breaking stride or changing directions, we stepped on board. We were greeted with friendly gestures, the ropes were released from their holdings and the River Queen slid out from the wooden pier. The well–muffled diesel engine started without hesitation. White bubbles burst from under the stern as we got underway.

I looked for the last time toward the dark-green domain of the gentle Pygmy people who live at peace with nature. Forget them? Never! For in my lifetime there are people I will forever remember. The Pygmies are some of them.

When I departed, I took with me something of what I saw and some of what I felt. And too, I hope I have left a modicum of myself for them to pleasantly remember.

That is the feeling I had when I went forward on our River Queen. I looked back toward the jungles remembering the Pygmies who were hidden so deep in the rain forest and the riverside village where we danced and enjoyed a lively evening.

Back in the states, we pump our own gas. We go inside to a busy clerk who says, "Which pump?" or "Thank you, have a nice day."

When checking out at a store or restaurant, the clerks very pleasantly repeat, "Cash or charge," or "Thank you," and "Have a nice day." I am not saying that is bad, but I have difficulty remembering the person if all I see is the top of the clerk's head.

In the native villages I never understood a native. I do not remember anything a native said, but I do remember the person. We had time to make eye contact, to see each other and to feel the goodness of another human being. That must have been the feeling of Shakespeare when he wrote, "Parting is such sweet sorrow."

The hunger pains I carried on board disappeared after devouring a good sandwich and a sack-full of fruit, which I took forward to the riverboat's bow.

Pulling a web-cushioned chair to just above and to the port side of the bowsman, I settled down for what I hoped would be an interesting ride. My thinking was that the bowsman not only checks the river's depth, but keeps an eye out for anything that may be interesting or obstructing our course.

There was a magazine article, including a photograph, of a giant serpent sticking his head and long neck out of the water on this very river. The missionary who reportedly took the photo also revealed the name local natives had given the serpent. I had no plans or desires to sit on the banks of Lake Loch Ness in Scotland with a camera in hand waiting for the water to boil just to get a glimpse of their monster, but as long as I was here, I might as well be ready for whatever popped its head up. As David must have thought when he slew Goliath, "It's a long shot, but I might as well give it a try."

On an underwater sand bar below the river dam in Ottumwa, Iowa, a log lodged and stuck its interesting head out of the water for all bridge travelers to see. I personally saw this thing of the deep and it certainly looked like the head of a dinosaur to me.

From his vantagepoint on the sand bar, he watched the traffic move past for weeks. Now, he not only was interesting, but also had a special personality. That serpent became the townspeople's favorite pet, and as days passed, he naturally obtained an appropriate name. Jim Hannann of the *Ottumwa Courier* took a close up photo, which made the front page and entered the archives of our history.

I, too, didn't want to miss out on photographing a chance sight of a greenish tree limb protruding through the river's surface, never knowing for sure if it could have possibly been the "Loch Ubangi Monster."

If all living things are somehow related, possibly our own river serpent's kin may pop his head up to look around again. If it had happened in front of the River Queen during the evening of December 30, 1974, his photo would be here for you to see.

Soon after the sun dropped from view beyond the western horizon, the moon's full hemisphere began casting its reflection from beyond the darkening green jungles in the east.

103

Other than the water splashing along the bow, all was quiet. During the darkness I watched for bonfires in villages along the riversides, but none were to be seen.

The map of the old Belgian Congo, now Zaire, shows three towns or cities on the river's eastern bank which we should have passed. Zongo, across from Bangui, could possibly still be a population center. However, the other two, Libenge and Dongo, no doubt, are abandoned and overgrown by the relentless jungle.

The hours traveling up river were long and tranquil. However, I never relaxed my vigil watching toward both shores.

Approaching Panama's Atlantic port at night while still hours out to sea, a voyager will see a world famous welcoming glow above the western horizon. Sea going sailors named it "The Crescent of Cristobal."

Approaching Bangui in the night's late hour, we saw no crescent over Bangui, not even a glow, but rather an incandescent light bulb reflecting off the yellowish painted building next to the wooden pier.

The only thing of beauty was the dancing yellow ribbon glittering its way out from below the security lamp's porcelain shade. The bulb's illumination, as small as it was, became our guiding light.

As our riverboat slowed to a crawl, she had finished a trip from Bangui down river to the Republic of the Congo and returned. I never heard her brush a sand bar or scrape a snag. Half of the voyage was at night without searchlights or buoys, just a boatman hanging over the bow taking depth and shouting back information. Watching may have been easier for the boatman during the moonlit night as the water's surface had turned to silver, making ripple watching more tranquil and obsticles less difficult to spot.

With a rub and a bump and a quick flick of their looped rope, a half hitch secured the River Queen to her port of original embarkation.

Saying and waving our final farewell, Sherm Cooper and I stepped onto the dock. I was carrying off what I had carried on, a camera and excitement.

XV

THE CHICKEN TWO-STEP
4 Degrees North – 18 Degrees East

The gate from the dock area was opened as we fired up our bikes to ride off into the city night. Before going five blocks, we met the headlights of two motorcycles. All of us stopped. It was two of our replacement riders from the Boston, Massachusetts area, Dick D'Ambrosia and Dick Bettencourt. Their body clocks were seven or eight hours out of sync with local time, so they had been out wasting time.

The four of us started riding together along a quiet, dimly lit street when my bike sputtered and died. I was out of gas. That was not the first time for me to run out of gas, but it was a first for being directly in front of the Emperor's palace gate. As soon as we knew the problem, we all commenced doing the chicken two- step. That's running around with our heads down, trying to find a beverage can in the darkness to transfer gasoline. The first person to find a can hollers, "Here's one." However, we all stopped before a winner was declared.

The Emperor's personal guards started charging down the long drive toward us. They didn't seem to be impressed with our rendition of the chicken two-step, as their big guns seemed to be pointing our direction. Rather than waiting to exploit our talents with an encore, we started falling all over one another pushing, pulling, running with our bikes and getting out of the light and into the darkness.

If the guards thought our dance routine was bad, they should hear us sing. (Through the years the four of us have become close friends, doing numerous things other than the two-step; and because of Sherm Cooper, the other three of us have joined him and Wally

Dalenback's Colorado 500 each September. The Colorado 500 is an invitational off road motorcycle Ride of Champions.)

While in the city of Bangui, we were told of one of the Emperor's atrocities. Some of the schoolboys apparently resisted wearing uniforms to school, as was their directive. The Emperor had those young men put into a holding cell. He, himself, personally went into the cell and clubbed many of the youthful boys to death. Just a few months after we were in Bangui, while the Emperor was visiting one of his tyrant cronies in North Africa, the French flew in a detachment of Foreign Legion troops forcing a coup d'etat.

On December 31 we left the city, passing their gates with little hassle. Bill Record and Jack Hawthorn had been trying everything, so I was told, up to, but not including, hijacking a barge to get us across the Ubangi River and into Zaire, but to no avail. What really happened in Bangui for the past three days only the other men know. Myself, I had the time of my life being a foreign witness to a Russian military operation, traveling hundreds of miles by boat and visiting an ancient culture.

As Jack was leaving Bangui, he and a small van nearly side swiped. All cleared except for Jack's left elbow. He never went down, but came to a rolling stop in appalling physical anguish with his good hand still on the bars.

Back at the mission in Bangui there was a doctor and her husband who were spending a few days there before going on to the desert nation of Chad. She was a doctor, just what our wounded needed, we thought. Not only was she a doctor but also as lovely as the flowers of Cuernavaca. With this in mind, Jack hurried back past the gates into the city to get his badly bent funny bone fixed. In two or three hours he came back with his left arm in an elbow shaped cast.

That's when he told us, "She's a digger, not a doctor." Her doctorate was in archeology. "But she certainly seemed to know how to fix this elbow."

This was probably the French couple who was kidnapped a few weeks later by a tribe in Chad. After one and one-half years of being held in captivity without pressure from the government of Chad, the French Foreign Legion flew in to gain their release. From news reports, it was not told whether the French secured the archaeologist's freedom with rifles or ransom. Nor did stateside news provide information on whether they had been physically abused or their condition at the time of their liberation.

Our camp was set up early that evening of December 31, 1974, and as usual, I left on my bike with a rope to obtain wood for the evening fire.

Protruding above the vines and other trees were the bleached silver-gray, upper limbs of a dead tree. This was my ultimate destination. However, along the way I rode slowly, looking for old dry wood that I could tie the rope onto and pull back for the evening bonfire.

While I was still riding slowly on this unused trail and watching both sides, a replacement rider from Montana overtook me. Jim Squires had been a Peace Corps worker for a few years in Brazil, and, as I saw later, was pleasant with the natives and greatly enjoyed communicating with them. This may have saved my neck.

When the natives realized where I was going, Jim was alerted to my peril. He started up his bike and rode hard through the brush and undergrowth to overtake me as I was riding slowly, still looking for dead wood. He let me know in no uncertain terms that there was a large animal trap near the dead tree. As we stood there together looking forward, not more than a hundred feet ahead was a slight depression. This was the vined-over, camouflaged cover of a large deep trap, big enough to catch and hold an elephant.

I appreciated Jim stopping me. I don't even want to imagine what entrapped reptiles lurked in the darkness of the pit.

With the setting sun, the year was done. By that night we should have been within Zaire, traversing their deep mud holes and ruts. Knowing Bill Record, our leader in a Third World environment, if the power of the dollar could have gotten us across the Ubangi River either by barter, wage or bribery, we would have been in Zaire.

Our group pauses at a village on the road to Bangassou.

XVI

VOLCANIC TOILET BOWL
5 Degrees North – 22 Degrees East

In five thousand miles of traveling Africa's roads, this was the first river we crossed by bridge. We had crossed a small stream or two plus the moat in Ceuta, but this was the first real bridge.

Soon after crossing the Totto River, we turned to the left going upstream to twin waterfalls. We parked near the big river's backwater above the cascades. As we walked over to the upper reaches of the falls, the sun was baking the sand foot-blistering hot. However, just as soon as we stepped onto the solid rock plate, even though it was seventy–five yards or so from the water, the deep anchored stone in the equatorial sun was cool to the touch.

Now I'm going to tell a story that I don't want to write, reread, or be reminded of again; but in the account of our trek across Africa, it needs to be told. I hope I can tell it in a manner as vividly as I still visualize.

As usual, we needed to take a bath, and why not here? On the topside of the falls the river had no banks. The flat rock gently descended into the water, which dropped straight down two hundred feet. Close to where the water dropped over the huge flat rock was a hole shaped like a toilet bowl. It was about three and one-half feet across and nearly four feet deep. Water flowed in from all sides at a very fast rate. In the bottom of the bowl there was a hole going down that was two feet across. This hole or tube that went straight down may not have been part of the water falls, but could have been a volcanic fissure caused by hot escaping gas from volcanic activity millions of years ago. If it were a volcanic fissure, the incoming water would drop into a subterranean cavity and not into the river exiting below.

What we were doing one after another was bathing in this natural toilet bowl. We would help each other in and help each other out. We had to keep our feet spread eagle to prevent them from going into the funnel's center hole, which was forced by the constant flushing of water persistently pounding downward on the feet.

I was second or third into the hole, and during bathing I really concentrated on keeping my feet pressed outward. I was really scared of slipping and going into horrible eternity. It was a quick bath and the fellows helped pull me out.

Three of us were around the edge when Del Haines went in to take what was nearly his fatal plunge. He was bathing and when he turned to rub soap over another area of his body, his right foot slipped. When he dropped downward, Jim Squires seized him momentarily as Don Murke and I grabbed onto his arm. We stabilized Del until he got his lost leg out of the hole. Then while he lifted himself, we pulled to get this fighting fugitive out of death's grip.

That's all I could take of playing Russian Roulette in a toilet bowl. I walked away in my swimming trunks and sneakers after picking up my camera, heading for something that could blow the past few minutes out of my mind.

Nearly numb from the frightful experience, I walked up to the very edge of a hundred fifty-foot cliff that paralleled the cliff between the two waterfalls. Not being able to see the face of the cliff I was above, but looking at the cliff on the far side as well as the cliff between the water falls, I knew what the one I was about to climb down was like.

Never have I been a rock climber, and I've always been afraid of heights. But at that moment, I was insensitive to my innermost feelings. Without fear I turned around, got on my hands and knees and backed over the fringe of the cliff. This was suicidal, for looking across the waterfalls, I knew I could only find toeholds in the plate rocks, and handholds if the roots were similar to the other sides. Keeping my face near the cliff wall, I kept feeling carefully while reaching for the next lower toehold that I could never see. Descending, one might as well have been blind, for it was totally touch and feel; find and hold. Near the lower reaches there were no more roots to grasp, but my fingers found solid outcroppings of rocks that gave me good places to cling to while finding yet lower and lower toe steps.

Stopping to rest and get my bearings, I looked over my left shoulder and downwards. Everything seemed fine except there appeared to be an undercut to the left. I moved to the right for security since there was no way to see beneath me.

Using total concentration, by the time I was on the lower level rock plate, I had completely forgotten the happening on the topside.

From this new location on the cliff, I began descending again. Slowly and one step at a time, with my fingers aching from clinging extra tight while feeling to find my next step, I finally reached a flat surface.

I then reached back with my foot before letting go with my hands, making sure I could step onto a real riverbank. I turned around for the first time and saw an entirely different world. It was then I realized the thunderous reverberation of a river dropping nearly straight down. To my back, of course, was the cliff, but facing south was a vast grass and water-covered river delta extending for miles.

From where I was standing, it was small and damp from the constant spray and very picturesque. The only indication of movement in the marshland below was the sun's sparkling reflection from the smooth shiny leaves and my knowing that creatures lurked just below the surface.

After seeing with amazement the drastic change below the falls, I was ready to see if climbing the cliff was going to be overly challenging now that my head was clear.

Because the stage was small, all that was visible upwards were the plates of rocks protruding from this nearly vertical bluff.

There may have been another way off around the edge, but I was going to try the vertical ascent. As it has often been said, the first step is the most difficult. But straight up a rock ladder? With toes forced into slots and fingers clinging to whatever seemed firm, I was on my way up.

Again, as coming down, it was necessary to keep my head and body close to the rocks as the finger-gripping places didn't have a grove to catch my fingertips.

Being by myself, it was extremely important not to make an error. Concentrating again on each step up, moving one limb at a time, I pulled gently with both hands and pushed with only a solid toehold.

One step and uplift at a time and I finally touched a root protruding above my head. The roots made good safe holds so I could pull myself while pushing with my feet. From there on it was a hundred times easier than when I was on rock only. Over the top, it was loose. But using all of my body, and feeling carefully for stones to hold fast to, one last pull and I was on flat rock. Eureka!

The cliff on the right is the one I descended and reclimbed to clear my mind.

XVII

FIRSTHAND ACCOUNT OF TRIBAL MASSACRE
5 Degrees North – 23 Degrees East

Coming into Bangassou, we performed our usual routine when entering a town for the first time, stopping at their police station to fill out their questionnaires and letting them know we were just passing through. The city still had one way traffic signs left over from the days of the Europeans and their hundreds of motor vehicles.

We stopped at the only retail establishment still doing business. It was a general store operated by an Irish couple. Inside the store neither the husband nor the wife would look at us. They only looked down while making change. It was evident these two white people, perhaps the only Caucasian family left, lived in fear. To prevent them from receiving repercussions for associating with these white outsiders, we purchased what we needed and left without lingering.

After leaving the general store and the Irish couple with whom I would have enjoyed exchanging information, we drove east through tree lined streets. A few years ago when the Europeans were there, it must have been a well–planned, beautiful city. Now the fine homes and streets were empty, and it seemed shadowy dark and depressing.

The street turned into a dirt road that disappeared into the jungle. Where the dirt road began, we turned right to the Ubangi River, a river we had desired to cross for the biggest part of a week. I had been on or near the Ubangi for six hundred and fifty miles, but this time it was a very different view.

We came to a stop on the bank that was the apex of a great river bend. From this strategic vantage point some nation had built a thick-walled brick battlement to

113

accommodate a cannon. It was an advantageous location to control river traffic. First of all, the channel was on the outside. Then there were long views in both directions. In addition, because of the low cannon angle, a cannoneer could water–skip a hot cannonball into a seaman's teacup.

So it was again. We were within sight of our next country to cross, but no closer getting there. Looking across this Mississippi-sized river, all we could really see was a dark green forest rising up and away on the far side. With the light reflecting off the water, we could not tell if there was a barge on the other side or not. The only way for us to know was to find a canoeist with his dugout to take some of us over there.

It was mid–afternoon when we set up camp near the banks of the Ubangi. We spent the afternoon trying to wash some clothes, checking out our tents for cuts, and Jack spent some extra time fixing a better meal. Repairs on the bikes weren't required, as we never had a breakdown. Since we were out of the desert now, we could go a few days between cleaning air filters.

Other than a half-mile of water with no way to cross, we didn't have a worry in the world. That is until during the night, an Iowa-type thunderstorm hit with full force, blowing hard with pounding rain and lightning flashing in every direction. The big, four-inch diameter, thirty-foot high bamboo shaves were crashing down around us, adding to the vibrant booming thunder and the crackling of lightning.

In the lightning flashes and beating rain of the electronic laser show of nature, it was confusing trying to distinguish who were the victims and who were the rescuers as we were out trying to untangle people, tents and jungle debris. Soon the storm passed and with a bruise or two we crawled back into our shelter, soaked and chilled, but to quote the final line of *Gone with the Wind*, "Tomorrow is another day."

Another day it was, bright and shiny. During the morning hours the rain's water had soaked away and it wasn't too muddy. However, there were bamboo and assorted limbs to clear from the area.

In many of our lives there is a day when we really need the visit of a minister. This must have been that day. For coming across the river in a dugout canoe, being paddled by a young boy from Zaire, was an English-speaking, Norwegian Baptist missionary. He not only was a representative of our Savior, but also a mode (to cross the river) that had eluded us in Bangui, four hundred and fifty miles back west, and so far here in Bangassou.

The missionary we met was a middle-aged, stocky built, outgoing fellow wearing a short sleeved shirt and slacks, the first casually dressed person we had seen since the Yamaha group back in Tamanrasset a good month ago.

With the meeting and greetings soon out of the way, the gist of the conversation turned to, "If you can help me, I can help you across the big river."

There wasn't enough love or money back in Bangui to get a barge to take us across the Ubangi River into Zaire, but now if we could get its engine started, there would be a barge from the other side of the river to use. No problem. Don Murk understood diesels and our support truck had a battery for cranking it up. So, if there were diesel fuel, we needed to start learning the river currents, as we were going to become sailors of the Ubangi.

What we were contemplating and completed in the following few hours was as illegal as shooting buffalo on Broadway, as crossing the Cold War Checkpoint Charlie while the East German guards were reloading. It was a fact. With no officials on either side to do our legal papers, we were going to leave the Republic of Central Africa and enter the nation of Zaire on our own. Not only were we letting ourselves out and into another country without their knowledge or permission, but we were using their own barge while perpetrating this transgression.

Have you ever noticed that when a group of people meet for the first time, even with a big job to be done, they enter into conversation before labor? So it was during this mid-morning encounter that this missionary told us his story with such clarity that I could see with vivid reality the cruelness man can inflict upon man. Not only did he relate to us his account of what happened, but he also showed the scars on his arms where he tore his own skin trying to break away.

There is an African proverb, "Human blood is heavy; the man that shed it cannot run away."

There never has been a reason for war, only excuses. The senseless war for the control of what was then the Belgian Congo came to this small community on May 28, 1965, by way of members of the Simbas tribe bent on a massacre.

The following is an account as told by Rev. Johannes Holte, a missionary and one of the survivors from a village in Equatorial Africa. Not unlike villages in most other regions of the world, good and caring people no doubt, inhabited it.

The sin of cruelty was perpetrated on each of the villagers and congregation by tying their knees together and their elbows together behind their backs. After all were bound and forced to kneel, an executioner with a machete began chopping their heads off, one after another, amid terrified, hysterical screams.

The missionary told us that when it was his turn to die, "God froze the arm of the executioner who then dropped the machete and ran." Opening his eyes after being petrified with the apprehension of the near demise of him and his wife, he saw amongst the human remains the machete. He was able to turn his back while lying down, to get his hands on the handle of the machete. He then scooted over to his wife and cut her loose so that she could free him and some of the remaining horrified souls.

The terrorists, apparently sickened from their own atrocities, didn't prevent him and his wife from escaping into the jungle. Whether or not the others escaped or were murdered, he either didn't look back to know, or if he did, he didn't mention seeing them again. What he did say was that he and his wife ran long and hard through a jungle trail, fearful they were being chased. When reaching near exhaustion, the two would hide in such a manner to watch the trail without being seen. The following day, still fleeing to safety, they encountered unexpected new companions. Their intended executioner and his teenage daughter overtook them as they, too, were escaping.

I do not believe God picks and chooses who will die by the sword and who will remain. I also do not believe this executioner realized the iniquity of his action. Rather, I believe, from a logical aspect, that this executioner, who was using a machete as a sword, was the political leader of that very village, and to save his own neck was forced by tribal butchers to personally kill his own people. For two reasons I believe this. The first reason is that his daughter must have lived nearby, as women do not travel with militants. Second, for the villagers to be in a group before capture, I would believe they were led by someone they trusted.

Be that as it may, now they were a foursome without basic necessities to live, such as food, water and shelter. He told us that even though working together, their chances of survival were fast diminishing and they had to return to a traveled road and take their chances. Virtually any group they could meet would be their enemies except one, and that was the very one which came along. A Belgian armed mobile patrol stopped for them.

Reverend Holte told of many firefights on the way back to a Belgian controlled city. There, heavily armed vehicles with a number of machine guns silenced any opposition that was encountered.

After spending a few years in Norway, he and his wife returned to the same place as before where they were so badly needed, spending forty years as missionaries until retirement.

XVIII

WE SEAMEN OF THE UBANGI
5 Degrees North - 23 Degrees East

We removed the battery from under the hood of Afro Annie and loaded it near the center of the dugout canoe that belonged to the Zairean boy. Ralph Hurtienne, Don Murk, and I, with the boy as the oarsman, started across the Ubangi River in what was once a tall, straight and for much of its trunk, a limbless tree. With nothing but a craftsman's skill and his chopping adz, it had been transformed into a long, true river conveyance.

The dugout was so sensitive to its passenger's movement that if his hair wasn't parted in the middle, this canoe wanted to capsize. In its defense, we had so overloaded it that on both sides the water was within a ripple of coming over the brim. By weighing her down so heavily, the canoe was transformed from a boat of transportation into a water-crossing pack mule, displacing over a third of a ton of human cargo and an irreplaceable battery. None of us could have been accused of being clever, or we would have fixed a flotation device and a line on our twelve-volt potential power source in case our long slim dugout decided to overturn.

Progress was slow, but constant as the young canoeist never broke the rhythm of pulling his oar through the yellowish brown water. Even though we had no choice with whom to cross the Ubangi, we had no qualms of this broad shouldered, quiet young man's ability to reach the far shore of one of the world's ten major rivers.

It may have been half an hour before nearing the Zairean shore where we could see a short wooden pier with a small barge secured alongside. What a sight after all this time to be approaching the barge that we were planning to confiscate for a few hours, hoping to bring all our equipment over from where it was sitting on the other side.

All that was necessary was to make friends with the natives. If we could accomplish this and board the barge without objection, it wouldn't take us long before we could find out whether or not this canoe crossing was in vain.

Never changing course, the youthful Zairean oarsman beached his boat in the same mud impression he must have left hours ago. With the dugout canoe still rocking, its bow stuck in the muck and her stern silently floating in the cloudy river water, it was at last a fact – we had reached Zaire.

I had been on and along this big river for six hundred fifty miles. I had been seeing its forest covered, distant, dark green shore for a week. Then at last, I could put my footprint on her eastern shore.

This land a few years ago was the Belgian Congo, where, no doubt, the native labor force was overworked and underpaid. Even with oppression, the community, industry and the individual had a purpose and a direction focusing into the future. With the war in the late fifties and early sixties there were hundreds of thousands of deaths resulting from Blacks killing Black and Black and White killing each other. The country gained its liberty but gained absolutely nothing but despair for virtually every Zairean, except for a small minority.

The winner was the soil that gained from the nutrients it absorbed from the decaying bodies of its victims. The soil is still winning the spoils, years after their war. Excluding a few cities, the only cure for disease is time and death. Leprosy, goiters, elephantiasis and whatever else that is contracted goes unchecked. Roads are impassable. Villages are isolated and are only as large as a water hole can support. I never saw a grave. The natives didn't even have shovels if they would desire to bury their deceased.

From drawings depicting the towns and villages, and from the descriptions in the early explorer's autobiographies, Equatorial Africa had an acceptable working culture.

A few years after the early exploration of the Dark Continent, buying and selling of the young and healthy blacks reached such a high volume that the total population of Africa was reduced dramatically.

After this shameful period came the colonists from Europe with differing degrees of harshness for suppressing and/or manipulating the people and their land. However, in doing so, colonizers built cities, developed plantations, mines and industry. They also exported their goods without just compensation.

With the conclusion of World War II, public opinion and pressure by many members of the United Nation countries forced colonists to relinquished control. Some colonial nations just pulled out, leaving Africa without technicians or government leadership. In some countries there were bloodbaths. Zaire may have been the worst.

Reaching Zaire, Don Murk picked up the support truck's battery. Ralph Hurtienne, the oarsman, and I left the dugout canoe. There were some twenty feet of soft mud and aquatic growth to walk and climb through before the bank leveled off as solid ground.

Crossing the Ubangi River successfully was just the first step in a long day's adventure. We had a delicate and difficult mission to accomplish. First, we had to be sure not to offend and to make friends with the local men. If no one objected, we would then walk onto the small wooden pier, letting the natives know our intentions. Then we would check out the barge, along with its engine, starting it up for a couple of round trips across this big river.

Fuel supply had been a topic of an occasional conversation since the Norwegian Missionary had let us know of a diesel powered barge that was tied up on this, the Zairean side. Even if all else went well, we certainly wouldn't care to run out of fuel in the river current and drift into an equatorial sunset. We walked about two hundred feet to the pier where three or four teenagers were enjoying being boys. After stepping up on the dock, we crossed over to the barge just as if we owned it.

The barge was a complete surprise in design, as it was built from what was available at the time. One thinks of a barge as being long and wide with a flat bottom. This one was two longboats, capable of carrying ten or twelve people each, positioned side by side and two feet apart. Planks were fastened crosswise the full length of these two boats to become the deck. The engine room consisted of a five-foot shanty with a gabled roof and a hinged back door. Inside this doghouse sized chamber was an oily power plant that, no doubt, had its beginning tucked neatly under the hood of a vehicle built for the road. Disappearing beneath its deck was the power shaft that we hoped would soon be turning the power screw.

With the propeller between the hulls, it was protected from cutting into mud or sand. However, with the twin vee hulls the barge drew nearly two more feet of draft than the typical flat bottom concept.

Don never looked around, but went directly to work checking out the engine, its drive and fuel supply. At last, after waiting for this chance, it seemed a time to hurry. Not only were there but twelve daylight hours near the equator to get our day's work completed, but the barge was small. We would have to make at least two round trips across the river to transport us and our units into Zaire. Also, the fellows who met us were young guys with no authority. If word got back to their leaders, we would need their blessing to pull off this water crossing.

Don was halfway inside the engine room when he shouted out, "Let's give 'er a try."

To me there is nothing pleasing about the sound of a diesel engine. They knock, rattle, belch and smoke, with no sound of authority.

Within a minute or two of Don's command, she started to knock and rattle, belching smoke with a vibration running across her wooden deck. The oily, cast-iron wonder was running. After making more checks for such things as fuel quantity, leaks, and anything that might be amiss, she seemed to be ship–shape.

121

Don idled the diesel engine back to engage the power shaft. This would be the final test. The engagement was made. Instantly bubbles and swirling current were foaming between the twin hulls. He pulled the rudder both left and right. This baby was ready to embark. Ralph pulled the planks that were used as loading ramps on board. I released the lines from the posts. This vessel with no name was drifting free.

After drifting out for a few minutes, she was shifted to forward at full port rudder and set a course just upstream from where we hoped to come ashore. That would be to the right of the cannonless fortification. With the current centered in the apex of the big bend, our plans were to progress slowly and drift down into the landing where our bikes and other riders were waiting.

I had spent enough time on rivers to know that unexpected sandbars or ridges of mud can catch a hull at any time. And with the vee hulls, our draft was deeper than on a regular barge. Snags are short, sharp, broken off tree limbs sticking out from water–logged tree trunks hidden below water level. If we would have hit a snag or if the engine would have quit, we would have had problems.

A week before, when Sherm and I were passengers on the boat from Bangie to the Republic of Congo, there was a river seaman hanging out from the bow checking depth with a line and weight. He, too, never took his eyes off the river, trying to see past the murky waters for an ambush set by the unpredictable currents.

If that river seaman didn't trust the riverbed, neither should we. Rather than full throttle and blind luck, we too had to use caution, the Braille system, touch and feel. I was the self–appointed lookout and I might as well have been blind. Hanging out front watching for something hidden from view by the clay colored water, I couldn't see anything to indicate a hazard, no white water or the telltale semi–circle waves of a boulder near the surface. We went slowly without variation of RPM's of our cast iron diesel that kept us moving forward.

I have forded dozens of rivers in motorcycle endurance races. Some I have crossed riding feet up and a couple I have floundered face down, but always with intensity and anticipation of impending disaster. This was peerlessly different. There was no intensity, just the unknown depth, crossing a wide river at what may be its lowest ebb of the dry season. With this unknown factor, the anticipation of hearing the sound of running upon a sandbar or ripping the side of the hull never took place. We crossed the calm side into the outer side of the big bend without an obstacle ever touching her hull. The power was backed off, letting her drift by the battlement. Then with a gentle run of the engine, we ran her aground on the Republic of Central Africa's river landing. It was a piece of cake. We just jumped onto the dirt bank with the lines, then secured her to a couple of shoreline trees.

Our gear had been packed. It was just a matter of getting loaded on the ever-moving barge. Within a half-hour we had as much as we thought she could carry on board and stowed down for another river crossing.

There were no government officials to stamp our visas and to fill out our necessary forms as we exited their country. As far as R.C.A. records would show, we are still in their nation. Bangasoo, near where we had been for the last two days, is no longer a city. It is merely an area where there are buildings and streets. A population center it is not.

Out there in the bush there are no government, no taxes, no law, except the personal law recognized throughout the world by reasonable and proper people. That is not to transgress upon another person or upon another person's property. In Republic of Central Africa where we were finally leaving, their village communities seemed to work in a primitive sort of way. Across the river nothing worked for the benefit of the human being.

We pushed the barge with no name toward the channel to start the return voyage. She had pulled another foot of draft, setting her really low in the water. The trip after this one would have nothing on board but our mother truck, Afro Annie. Even with our truck as empty as we could get her, we could well have had the barge drafting past her limit. If the Dodge Power Wagon overloads her, it would be just a matter of stripping the wagon down and making an extra crossing.

Looking across the Ubangie again, all you could see on the far off shore was the dark green jungle of the river's bluffs. Between the far riverbank and us was a half-mile of shallow near currentless murky water. It's this slow moving muddy water that drops its silt into mud bars that wait hidden under the surface of the water to catch an unsuspecting hull that may attempt to pass over.

Not one of our riders ever used the term, "what if." Crossing this Mississippi-sized river, we could have found that phrase quite appropriate many times over. However, the people who use the words "what if" were safe at home. Our men were a melting pot of different backgrounds. They may or may not have been lacking in a number of qualities, but two qualities they all excelled in were courage and a driving desire to move on.

No one wanted to have the hull ripped out by a snag, to run aground or to have the engine quit midstream. But these concerns were never voiced. We weren't a bunch of reckless dummies. We used every precaution we had at our disposal. After all, by then we had an hour of practical knowledge as seamen of the Ubangie, in addition to my expertise at river crossings on my endurance bikes.

Another rider and I took this limited practical knowledge to the bow of the barge and watched for swells or color change at the water's surface.

Don pushed the throttle forward. The little cast-iron diesel rattled and knocked as she was given left rudder heading her up stream past the old battlement's fortification. Trying to retrace his first course, Don pulled a nearly ninety-degree, right-rudder heading toward the dark green Zaire riverbank.

With the total green shore and the sun's reflection off the water, it was impossible to see a sighting for a navigational reference point. Don kept her slow and straight from the heading he chose from the last turn in the channel. We never took our eyes off the water, as we were alert to a water change of about twenty-foot dead ahead. To miss seeing an underwater hazard could mean an abrupt end to our voyage.

Halfway across someone yelled, "There's the boat dock, straight ahead and a bit to the left." From years of fording rocky rivers on a dirt bike, self–taught discipline meant never breaking concentration by looking up.

Time passed as the anticipation increased. I became sure we were going to make it, even though the barge's twin hulls were pulling at least three-foot of draft.

The little diesel shut down. I looked up again, and there it was. The gray–white bleached wooden dock lay just ahead.

On and near the dock were the same shirtless, shoeless, capless boys as when we left. There were no hard-faced old guys with bad attitudes and low opinions of white intruders who steal their barge while only the kids are looking.

She bumped a bit hard with all her motorcycle cargo on board. I jumped onto the landing pier with its lines and secured her tight, then with a quick step back on board, kick started my XL250 Honda to life. When the planks went down, I rode off the deck and planted my tire tread deep into the black riverbank.

Not only was this river crossing a successful challenge, but also within my inner feelings I had a vindictive attitude against the circumstances which caused our delay. Hitting that riverbank hard and denting her soil deep gave me a feeling of equalizing a wrong, like hitting a brick wall with your fist. It's only the fist that hurts, but inside you feel better because of it.

So it was, January 5, 1975.

There was another trip or two to make across the Ubangie. I had crossed her three times in the last few hours. I didn't want to go back or even look toward the jungle that was waiting for us, so I stayed with my bike. The bike was nothing but alloy and iron, but for the past seven weeks, I had lived with her and slept beside her. I knew her like the back of my hand. She was my security blanket, my way through the jungles ahead. Somebody needed to stay with the bikes and befriend the native boys. I wanted to be one of them.

The nameless twin hulled wonder departed again for another load, including Afro Annie. With the bikes on the Zaire side all topped to the brim with gasoline, a few extra Jerry Cans full of our petrol, we felt if the support truck slid off into Davey Jones' Locker, at least we had wheels and extra gas.

Hitting that riverbank hard and denting her soil deep gave me a feeling of equalizing a wrong.

XIX

THE TRIAL – FACING JUNGLE JUSTICE
5 Degrees North – 23 Degrees East

With the barge returned and left as we found it, after bidding good–bye to the fellows who helped make this river crossing possible, we were ready to start inland.

Instead of going inland, the dirt track stayed in the flood plain, paralleling the river, soon hidden by trees. After a half-mile or so the track turned left, away from the river and up and over a line of hills. We started to ride through our first Zaire community. As we rode into the village, a Zaire soldier met us. He was a well-built fellow wearing a tan military uniform. He had very black skin and shiny, white teeth. All he needed besides an audience was a white handkerchief in his left hand and a trumpet in his right to be a Louis Armstrong look-alike.

He didn't want us to continue, but rather to set camp where we were, on the track across from their village. He also showed us he wanted our tents lined up in military fashion. The same was true of our bikes, one straight line all facing the clearing that was half surrounded by huts. I suspected that he knew he was supposed to stop people when they came through the village but didn't know the reason for this action.

So, we were again setting up camp early in the afternoon when the local boys came over to earn some RCA money by taking our Belstaff riding suits to a rocky river nook to beat the dirt out of them. We were doing our chores around camp while the soldier went back to being the King Fish. I'm not saying this Zaire G.I. was a ladies' man, but considering the smiles on the women's faces, I'd wager the first thing that wears out on his uniform would be the zipper on his pants.

In the weeds behind our camp were an old corncrib and an old frame of a truck that had been destroyed and stripped during their war. Neither was of any value. All the people had grown since the war were corn and babies. Both were short-lived. In fact, the former was already extinct.

Over in the middle of this village clearing was a log, maybe a foot in diameter and at least ten or twelve feet in length. Little did we realize that within hours this log and three of our men would be the center of attraction in a highly emotional controversy.

There wasn't much activity that evening except when the King Fish with his million-dollar smile took a kid by the elbow and wrist in a strong-arm manner, lifting straight up until the kid's bare feet barely touched the ground and put him in the corn crib. I don't know if the King Fish was just putting on a show for us or if the kid did something wrong, like looking where he shouldn't or eating a non–circumcised banana.

That nightlife may have been on the lighter side, but come morning we faced the harsh reality of offending these people and facing the possibility of native justice.

With the morning light, the day started peaceably with no indication as to when the soldier would let us continue on our way.

Near our camp was an old truck frame, a rusting-out piece of junk. But to the natives, it may have been something of more value. Possibly it was a memorial to their fallen dead, a testimonial to a hard-fought victory or maybe it was simply their possession and to take from it without asking or paying was considered stealing. We will never know.

The trouble started when one of our replacement riders by the name of Bettencourt, who had just joined our group a week earlier, decided to repair a broken grab handle on his bike by inserting a shackle bolt from this old truck frame.

Dick Bettencourt, in his ambitious hard working style, never was one to look back, whether dirt riding or wrenching. His motto always seemed to be "Go for it!" What he went for this time greatly offended one of the local men.

This man in appearance was different from the others. His antics may have made him look tall and aggressive, but the hat he was wearing really set him apart from the others. What he had on his head looked like an inverted cone, made from the leaves of reeds, which grow next to inlets along the river. These long, narrow leaves were bunched together at the top and tied, leaving a short tassel. Around the crown the leaves were cropped evenly and woven to form a fitted headband.

The hat was the only thing interesting about this person. When he saw what Bettencourt was doing, he became outraged, running into the village waving both arms high above his grassy headpiece. He shouted until he attracted the village crowd, bringing attention to the perpetrator of an alleged jungle crime.

Out of the crowd a runner left at full speed. The significance of this action can be summarized by one seven-letter word, trouble.

The hostilities did not diminish, as the throng of natives kept growing in size, until Bettencourt was surrounded by what appeared to be everyone within hearing range.

I kept watching the horde grow, looking in the direction the runner had gone, knowing sooner or later trouble would arrive. Sooner it was, but in double. Not only did King Fish join the accuser, but with him came their chief. They went directly to the shouting, arm waving, antagonistic adversary of this Bunch of North American Adventurers, who within the last twenty–four hours had commandeered a barge, left one country illegally, entered another illegally, and were now facing the wrath of hell for stealing an old rusty bolt.

This loud conference could be considered the meeting of a grand jury deciding if there was enough evidence for a trial and a conviction.

Each of us stood with dry mouths, sweaty palms and frozen faces awaiting their next move, now that all of those in authority had been informed of what the runner said had happened.

A group approached and wanted three of us. They didn't seem to care which three. Three of our men went forward with them to the center of the clearing to sit on their ceremonial log and face downward. The rest of us stayed on the side of their human ring, sitting on the ground, facing the gray, grassless soil.

The fresh, new day had turned into darkness and despair. We were at their mercy watching three of our buddies bowing over in the midst of loud, arm waving jungle men who were moving about, seemingly shouting insults and accusations.

This we knew was as fair as it was going to be, dispensing justice with the examination of the fact by emphatic jeering and yelling at each other. It seemed anybody could join in to be part of the judicial body. The only thing any one of us could see was our own boots and the gray trampled dirt between them.

No one looked up as it is a universally known law never to look your adversary in the eye except from a position of power. Power we did not have. When we shut down our engines the day before, we lost all semblance of power. But in the jungles of Zaire there is only one way to go, and that's in peace. It would be impossible to make a run for it as there was only one track through the jungle, and that track always ended at a river, which would take hours, at best, to cross.

I felt that day as I did when we were lost in the Sahara, sick from the possibility of impending doom but with no regrets since I had departed from my home with the love of each member of my family. And my business was in order.

I love an adventure and the unknown, but this had turned into a personal vendetta where someone would lose and be hurt. If the native in the hat and his followers (if any) lost, I had no idea if there would be ramifications that would befall him. However, if we lost, I knew of jungle justice. A person can leave his belongings in the middle of a village and nothing will be stolen, for those who have seen or heard about their punishments will never forget. I have heard, I remembered and felt sick.

My thoughts rambled to why they hanged horse thieves and cattle rustlers in the early West. The same conditions existed here. They had no jails and punished as needed. The loud yelling back and forth in a native tongue never declined as my perception of what was happening was totally wasted. I could think of no plans, nothing constructive. I just sat, looking between my knees and at times listening intently to pick up a trend.

Time passed as the intensity of the wild screaming had diminished to a point that I was ready to chance a look to see what had changed in the past half hour of our trial. At my first look I saw, still waving his arms, the accuser with the hat, trying to keep a crowd. My buddies were looking down; none of them were moving. It was imperative for me not to offend our accusers any more by provoking an individual while looking around before the trial was over.

I had been careful to keep my head facing down and by not letting my head move sideways. In other words, I let my eyeballs do the walking. It came to a point that the guy with the hat could no longer retain an audience.

The sickness began to leave my stomach. In apparent frustration this intimidating buffoon had run his course when, to the last village person, they all had turned their backs to him. This clown with the grass teepee for a hat, who so over–reacted because of an old rusty bolt, disappeared from my view. I never saw him again. I'm certain he tried with the utmost of his oratorical ability to turn the villagers into a violent mob against us. The goodness of these simple native people prevailed over the riotous encouragement from a vengeful bigot.

Our men retained their nearly frozen position for some time before moving. However, to our right side a conspiracy to defraud, one of many stages of drama in human life, was beginning to unfold.

A line, "What evil lurks in the minds of man?," from the 1940 radio program *The Shadow* came to mind. Approaching with evil lurking in their minds, positive attitudes for success and the desire of snake oil salesmen to line their pockets, were the two co–conspirators with their profitable proposal. The King Fish and his buddy, the local chief whom we were meeting personally for the first time, had a lucrative plan. They suspected that we had left the Republic of Central Africa with RCA money. They had gathered the "Zaire," money of Zaire, and we would exchange our RCA money for their Zaire currency.

It seemed logical. They could cross back over to Bangasoo to the Irish couple's general store and use the RCA money. We could go forward into the interior of Zaire and spend the Zaire money.

This we did, and all seemed well. Then we fell for another of the King Fish's bogus stories and took him with us.

XX

THE NIGHT OF THE SCREAMING JUNGLE
5 Degrees North – 23 Degrees East

It was nearly midday or early afternoon when we left the native village. I looked and hesitated before leaving. Every person was playing his typical part in the aftermath of the morning's drama. The kids were acting like kids; adults like adults. Missing was the buffoon in the hat made of grass, the one who could have cost one or more of us our lives. Which, to say the least, would have created the low ebb of our Africa Trek. There was no way of knowing whether this adversary of ours had become a martyr or a goat.

Departing this village was the end of the beginning of our arduous journey across a nation that was dying within itself. Beautiful or a squalid disfigurement, much of Zaire in the heart of Equatorial Africa was home for the hopeless, a people who had only each other in sickness and in adversity. They were harvested into slavery and/or taken advantage of, then abandoned into self–preservation. Beauty was in nature and rarely seen in the face of the native people.

The trail we traveled was south through tall, yellowish and light green grass. Within three or four miles the trail turned east toward a forest wall of trees and vines.

Within those trees there must have been a totally abandoned city, which a large population of Europeans inhabited until the late 1950s. There wasn't positive identification, but either this or the next abandoned city must have been the city of Ndu.

There was but one piece of evidence to support this conclusion. Next to the tree line, but still in the grass, stood a beautifully constructed, magnificent Catholic Church, an adjoining parsonage and a much-used public well.

It would have taken a large, well-funded congregation to construct such impressive buildings. Both the yellow clay bricks and the mortar they used were of excellent quality. The corner lines and walls were perfectly plumb, the mortar lines true, indicating construction was by highly experienced expert craftsmen. This evidence seems to be overwhelming as to the size of the city.

The houses of worship for the natives fit more closely to what they could tithe and are very suitable, I'm sure, in the eyes of the Lord. Mainly they consist of two or three rows of poles supporting a thatched roof and a raised pulpit with rows of pews made from planks set on cross logs.

The most heavily used path to the well was from the west, an indicator of a native village nearby in the bush. We took advantage of such an excellent source of water, filling all of our containers to the brim before moving on.

From there we left the influence of the great Ubange River and drove directly into the jungles of Zaire.

We have all been in places where the environment wasn't as we expected, but as we passed through trailside villages and seeing the people, we found ourselves totally unprepared. The initial shock of meeting individuals face to partial face or seeing persons with baseball size growths coming out from their necks nearly made me nauseous. Never had I seen leprosy or external goiters until I encountering these unfortunate individuals as I idled my bike through these tiny spots in Africa.

In our church we have minutes of silent prayer where I remember these unknown afflicted ones. The ones I saw have passed on now, hopefully for the better. However, others have taken their places in this desperate plight of ill-fated circumstances where enjoyment of life may be only a precious few moments.

By the third village compassion overcame shock, allowing me to exchange smiles which brought pleasure to them and me. From that village on, no matter how a person looked I exchanged my best smile with a hand wave and a loud, "Hi, there."

By luck, in the evening there was a clearing on the left side of the trail. Beyond the clearing was a large open area of jungle, as much as ten acres, a perfect place to set up camp.

At the clearing entrance was a twenty foot high vineless tree with a long wooden or bamboo cylinder suspended high from its limbs. We didn't know what it was, but our guesses were a burial crypt for a small person's body or a bird or monkey trap. By morning's hot sun we saw what it really was, a man-made beehive.

We no more than started setting up camp when the King Fish, who was riding in the support truck with us, left to hoof it back to the village we had recently passed.

Do you suppose he had an inclination there could be one or more love-starved ladies who would enjoy the company of a big boy in a flashy army uniform? Could be, for when he walked in to camp the next morning his shining black face was horizontally bisected by a grin ear to ear exposing his glossy, white teeth in a triumphant smile.

By the time our evening chores were finished, it was nearly dark. I started my bike's engine and proceeded to ride the jungle clearing in a clockwise direction near the outside perimeter. About two-thirds of the way around, in fact, directly across from our camp, I flushed a dozen guinea hens into a narrow animal trail at the jungle edge. Marking the place, I went back to get a flashlight and asked if anyone wanted to volunteer to go with me.

Ralph Hurtienne jumped at the chance to do some nighttime bird hunting in the jungle. This was our plan. Those guineas, because it was night, would soon find a place to settle down. Anticipating, our plan was when we found their roosting place we would return to our camp and make two snares from bamboo poles using wire as the snare loop. Then we planned to return to the sleeping, roosting guineas, slip the loop over their neck, give the wire a jerk and presto, we'd have a meal extraordinaire.

135

Ralph and I, each with flashlights, proceeded down the jungle path where the guineas entered. We searched every limb on both sides and overhead very slowly, not only looking for the fat gray birds, but protecting ourselves from being forced into a wrestling match with a long, powerful constrictor. We also wanted to avoid playing "suck the venom out" after an encounter with one of the little snake's "lucky strike."

Knowing this was an animal trail, we kept focusing the light beam up the trail looking for the telltale reflective dual eyes of a cat moving into position to catch the mouse.

We kept moving in, way beyond where I thought the guinea hens would be perched. Those birds are like chickens. Their eyes focus sideways and can't see at night. I didn't panic them and was sure they would be just ahead.

It was about that time that one of our fellows from the edge of the clearing could be heard screaming "Cats" at us. Slowly we turned, starting back using the flashlight, trying to maintain a complete circle of safety. Again he screamed, "Cats!" Natives were pointing toward where we entered. Reluctantly we retreated to the safety of the grass clearing, not knowing where the guineas had perched or if the natives really thought we were in danger.

Later that night, sitting outside my tent, I heard a wild scream. In another direction I heard another identical wild scream, and in a third direction, the same. With that, the jungle came alive with millions of insects, birds and animals. Anything that can make a noise must have emitted their highest decibel in total three hundred sixty degree stereophonic sound.

The intensity of the resounding resonance continued unobstructed for about a half-hour. Then, as if all power was shut off, it became instantaneously silent throughout the jungle.

Ten to twenty minutes went by. Again, in the silence of the night there was a wild scream, identically echoed from other directions. As before, a million voices, rubbing wings and with a multitude of unknown methods, the jungle again came alive.

It may not have been only the sounding of the creatures of the jungle and nearby swamp creating the high degree of stereophonic entertainment.

In the dampness of the night, the clearing with the wall of tall vine–covered trees possibly worked as a reflecting screen. A reverberating effect may have compounded everything we heard.

By the third number of this noisy symphony, I had quit thinking and started enjoying the conclusion of a day whose sequel I would never want to experience.

In the security and seclusion of my tent I again dropped off to sleep, at peace with the world.

XXI

CORRUPTION IN ZAIRE
4 Degrees North – 22 Degrees East

Going to sleep was to the melodic lull of the living jungle; awakening was into total silence until voices and rustling of our own men brought back life's reality. By the time we broke camp and were ready to leave, the King Fish came strolling through the clearing's ankle-high, grassy vegetation. He, no doubt, spent the night exchanging lice and passion with one or more of the consenting ladies in the nearby native village. His excuse or pretense for hitching with us was getting his back pay in Bondo where there was a small military outpost.

After passing the tree with the high beehive, we turned left down the long, narrow, dirt road toward Monga. It was near midday when we arrived. Monga was another city that yielded to the jungle's natural relentless impulses to overtake and smother anything in its way, when not held in check.

As an example of the power of the smothering jungle vines, in Central America countries I have seen large, tall trees that were wrapped by three to four inch thick vines and smothered to death. After the tree dies, the termites devour the dry wood, leaving a tree in appearance only. The trees become thick-walled, hollow tubes with a sparse scattering of leaves.

There is one such tree adjacent a playground in Monte Verde, Costa Rica. The children scoot up the hollow tree approximately a hundred feet. The bravest reach the top, sticking an arm out of slots between the vine's trunks, yelling to get attention for their courage.

We stopped in front of a cement walled building covered in vines except around an open door. Before us sat a small rectangular table.

The King Fish left, but soon returned with three of his comrades. We were then informed that we must show all the Zaire money we had. One at a time they absconded every Zaire cent from each of us, explaining this money was obtained illegally. I objected within myself to these actions. However, there was no alternative but to pay up. In the jungles of Zaire we were always trapped between the rivers.

It makes a person pause in wonderment. Is there a college of corruption somewhere for those with authority around the world? Or are their minds just perverted from the stench of association with their own kind?

The King Fish gave up his white toothy grin and sat along with his cohorts in front of the door at the weather stained table. The money was folded neatly and put away. At least it wasn't divided for all to witness.

Across the unused street was a gently rolling city park. The grass was uncut. The untrimmed trees, which years ago had each of their lower trunks painted white, were bleeding back to the gray color of bark. Using a lawn mower and a few hours of tender loving care, this little green woodland could be transformed back to a pleasant plaza.

Within the hour that we were detained, a large crowd of men had gathered in the park. They were a pathetic bunch, just standing nearly motionless without audible conversation, their eyes watching our every move. With those apparent willful looks, they may have had hopes we were returning Europeans to again bring industry to this town. There wasn't employment for livelihood and no stores remaining for them to buy anything if they had had spendable money, resulting in these people having only dingy, ragged clothes. Some wore T-shirts with a likeness of their president, Mobuto, printed on them. But they were nearly rotted past recognition.

This was the aftermath of their war for independence: a war they won through blood shed and public opinion. The spoils of victory were the loss of employment, industry and utilities. However, they gained their independence. In doing so, the people were forced for self-preservation to live in the jungle where they could hunt, gather and obtain water at any source.

It was written by Eric Hoffer in *The True Believer*, "Unless a man has the talent to make something of himself, freedom is an irksome burden." It was also written in Dorothy Bussy's 1902 writing *The Immoralist*, "To know how to free oneself is nothing; the arduous thing is to know what to do with one's freedom."

A mature-aged woman who looked as though she had toiled since childhood slowly walked through the standing crowd. Balanced on her head was a heavily laden basket. On her upper torso she was wearing a dingy, tattered, overly–worn T-shirt. Across its front, diagonally printed in French, was the word *Liberte*.

For a compassionate person, observing the futility of these people is pathetically saddening.

India's Mahatma Gandhi wrote, "The cause of liberty becomes a mockery if the price to be paid is the wholesale destruction of those who are to enjoy liberty." This is quoted from *Non-Violence in Peace and War*.

In America our forefathers fought and died to create and then retain our union. I will never forget that it was America's good fortune to be blessed with a mostly honest colonial leadership bonded by a common language. Also the French at that time were continually biting at the heels of the British. Consequently America survived and prospered through colonialism and eventual independence.

In Zaire all they received from their revolution was death, devastation and a bunch of political T-shirts; no soap, no water, just a bunch of T-shirts.

Leaving this town was similar to graduating from college. We were broke but had gained an education. With no spendable money and what turned out to be nineteen more days of traveling daylight until dark, we were on the move again.

The soldier we called the King Fish turned his back, never bidding Farewell to his fellow travelers. He knew he cheated us, and we were not his friends. He pulled a scam and played it to the hilt. The winner is the one who can enjoy the experience. The loser is the one who becomes bitter from greed or from dwelling on being fleeced.

In those two days from the Ubangi River we traveled nearly sixty miles. The King Fish would be on foot for those same miles if he returned to the village, the site of the trial, above the Ubangi.

Past the park we turned left gradually descending, then turned right, soon reaching the Bili River's north bank. Nine men, apparently from the park, must have walked to the river and crossed by dugout canoe; as we came to a stop, a barge was ready to leave the eastern shore to ferry us across this silent river.

Soon after shutting down our last motorcycle engine, we became aware of the rhythmic percussion of a drum. The river, being only two hundred yards in width, allowed us to observe the barge leaving its mooring. The barge came out from the far shore then turned itself ninety degrees to crosswise. Suddenly I could see the flat deck with drop ends riding on three long boats.

Now that's not unusual, but these men on board were silent. With a crew of six oarsmen, two using wide end mud ores, in addition to the drummer keeping everyone in perfect synchronization, the flat topped barge not only crossed the river but again turned itself ninety degrees and beached dead on at the landing site. This normally may not be a noticeable accomplishment. However, there was not an audible voice command, just the rhythm from the drum. All the oarsmen faced backward, pulling or pushing their ores. It was the drummer who faced forward and had full control of the barge by changing the beat.

We loaded, the first of two round trips. I sat on my bike amazed at the performance of the oarsmen. When the drummer finished his first chord, the six paddles dipped and pulled hard. The mud oarsmen leaned heavily on their poles. With that we moved out from shore. When the tempo of the beat quickened, the oarsmen stopped pulling forward, but inward and outward in short strokes until the barge's three longboats used for buoyancy had turned ninety degrees for the voyage to the far shore. Again the beat of the drum was in slow rolls, maintaining a rhythmic pull by the oarsmen in what seemed to be perfect unison.

Not only were we being transported; we were witnessing a concert such as no other, deep in Equatorial Africa. Instrumentation was by the oars, the dip, long pull through the water, the exit from the water. The lead instrument was a primitive drum.

These men, too, were without facial expressions, remaining vocally silent in the same manner as the men who watched us only a couple of miles back in the old city park.

Either in awe of or respect to the artist, we sat on our bikes in quiet wonderment, watching the boat being maneuvered in the river current. It turned and docked by a rat-a-tat, rat-a-tat, dip, swoosh, splash, dip, swoosh, splash. As the tempo changed, the angle of the ore blades changed, and the back pulls remained in rhythmic unison. With the last rat-a-tat, rat-a-tat, she docked as softly as the touch of Charmin.

XXII

FACING THE SHARP END OF A SPEAR
4 Degrees North – 22 Degrees East

The impressive sandy trail through Zaire's jungle was a continual flow of turns as the track serpentined past massive untouched trees. That morning ride was refreshing and tranquil. I never expected the dramatic change, from serene to terror, caused by the itchy trigger finger of my camera hand.

Coming up in front and to my left was an opening in the jungle. Beyond the trees and vines was a cotton field. This cotton field was not unlike the one I saw in the moonlight a few nights before.

When seeing the first one through an opening between the trees, it looked to be acres of a silver white field of bright deep snow reflecting from the moon's rays. That night I had no idea what it was I saw so I made a "U" turn and went inside the field. Using my headlights, I was totally surprised to see a field of cotton, which had ripened and burst. I knew the old cotton field would never be picked. There was no transportation, no market and no reason "to pick dat cotton."

This time I was going to get on film a photo of an old cotton field with millions of pods exposing their glowing white outgrowth.

I hadn't seen a native all morning and didn't have an inkling anyone was near when I stopped my bike and got into a position to get a well-balanced picture. Raising my 35mm single lens reflex to my eye, I started rotating my lens to bring the subject into focus. Looking through the lens I saw not a cotton field, but a blade, a fist, an arm and a dark body. The blade wasn't stationary but jabbing back and forth toward my face.

143

Not to make any quick moves I slowly lowered the camera and found myself facing a spear-wielding native. Rather than kowtowing by lowering my head and backing away, as I should have done, I chose the dumb alternative, accepting his threat as a challenge.

We were facing each other a mere twenty feet apart. I was at the edge of the narrow road, and he was standing between rows of cotton where he had been hiding as I approached on my motorcycle. The native would draw the long spear back and jab it toward me in an aggressive gesture. I, in turn, stared at the motion of the spear and kept a side to side movement, not making any gestures, but ready to dodge his flying spear if and when he threw it.

My actions of accepting his challenge infuriated the native to such a degree that he jabbed the blunt end of his long spear into the ground behind him. At that point he brought his body forward in a catapult position. All of his muscles bulged, the neck tendons protruded like external ropes. I froze where I stood. Never have I faced death face-to-face from another human being. I could no longer defend myself, as I became horrified.

I've heard stories of catapulting a spear entirely through the neck of a cow. There was no possibility of dodging a catapulted spear. My eyes went out of focus; my muscles were useless.

Behind me I heard a screaming voice but I never felt the sting of penetration. As my eyes focused again I saw between us a native leader wearing on his head a beanie of authority, yelling at the spear-wielding native. Three or four native boys ran up to look at me.

The native leader must have explained that my camera was nothing to fear. After a moment of conversation between the two of them, the native pulled his spear out of its aggressive position and fixed it standing straight up in the ground. He then walked over to a partly filled basket of cotton and proudly placed it in a balanced position on his head.

I must have been scared stiff. My arms felt like lead, my hands shaking, for it took some effort to bring my arms up with the camera to get their picture.

Because of the leader's quick action, I truly believe he prevented the native from becoming a "widow maker" for which I'll be forever grateful.

The bamboo jungle

XXIII

NEGOTIATING THE BAMBOO JUNGLE
4 Degrees North – 22 Degrees East

Much of Zaire is bamboo swamps. To cross this part of the country a dirt road had been cut through from the Ubangi River crossing at Bangassou to Kisangani (old Stanleyville) to carry produce during the dry season. Because the Europeans had departed, the road had reverted back to a track through the jungle. However, the wheeled vehicles passing through must have become stuck deeper and deeper until the holes were as much as five-foot deep. There were not just a few, but a multitude of holes appeared on and off again for miles.

It was a piece of cake for our XL250 Hondas to ride the edge of the mud hole ridges, but for Afro Annie, our support truck, it involved a process of drive in and cable winch out.

For two or three days in the bamboo swamps we were in the same proximity of two people and their bicycle. This couple was apparently leaving the jungle for a better life in the city and carrying all of their possessions, including a kerosene lantern and a shotgun, on their bicycle. The native couple never rode the bicycle, only pushed it loaded down with their belongings.

When the trail was without deep holes, we would get a good lead on the couple. However, when we reached mud and yellowish water-filled holes, it took us hours to get through. Then silently the native folks would pass us, again still pushing their heavily laden bike.

To transverse those deep bogs of mud we would stop Afro Annie and free up the winch at the front of the truck. A few feet of cable were run out, then pulled back over the hood. Bill Record would drive the truck down into the muck as far as she would go without digging holes if the tires spun. That is when my job began. After parking my bike, I would tie one end of a rope to the cable hook and the other end of the half inch thick hemp rope around my waste and start walking down the track looking for the closest bamboo cluster to anchor the support truck winch cable.

This area of Zaire was all bamboo jungle, covered with water and saturated plant life. However, there was a way over the water, getting only the feet and lower legs wet in the murky water. As the bamboo clusters keep growing new shoots from the inside, the oldest, largest bamboo shafts on the outside of their cluster had fallen over, leaving a mat of floating bamboo on which to walk.

I would find a small bamboo cane pole to use as a walking and balancing stick before starting out over the water. The shafts would always roll or sink more as I walked dragging the hemp rope, but I always found a makeshift causeway to a large, strong bamboo cluster.

After reaching the cluster, which would be about four-foot in diameter, I would tie the hemp rope around the cluster and pull the steel cable out to where I was, hook the cable around the bamboo to start winching the truck through the deep mud holes.

As the slow truck's electric winch pulled the cable taut, it squeezed tight around the bamboo cluster. The bamboo shafts would crackle, rumble and squeak, but it never loosened or even broke through the walls of the four-inch diameter bamboo shafts.

I would do my balancing act walking back out to the truck. The big Dodge truck would scrap and growl as it was pulled sideways through the deep holes.

Day after day we repeated the same show. Our skill factor never improved; the wench never broke; and the Dodge never died.

XXIV

EL TORO AND THE VIKING
4 Degrees North – 22 Degrees East

Don Murk was down, but not out. He raised himself up on one elbow and a straight arm. His lower body still sprawled out in a horizontal disarray. Indubitably, his "bell had been rung" to such an extent that the brain's automatic lower body control system was temporarily deactivated. As for his Honda, it was at rest at the conclusion of a few parallel scrape marks.

Shutting my bike engine off and stopping nearby, I hollered his name and the natural questioning cliché, "Don, what in the world happened?"

This narrow road, rarely if ever used, had a smooth sandy surface, making the absolutely finest riding conditions. But my new friend from Minneapolis was stunned, resembling a prizefighter who had just been K–Oed in the famous square ring.

Don, still forgetting he had legs, pointed toward his opponent. His opponent, still ferociously mad, some hundred feet or so away, stood facing us. He was ankle deep in a dry, grassy no man's land. His head was lowered, horns protruding outward from either side of his flat skull. With his front legs set wide, there was no difficulty in interpreting the body language of the enraged one-- Don't tread on me!

Don's reply wasn't that of a formidable competitor but that of a man who had met his match and was ruthlessly defeated. Pointing off to his left, the tanned, nearly two hundred-pound Minnesotan replied, "You see that black bull? I hit him right across the shoulder and crashed. He turned on me and charged."

Still trying to get up, Don Murk pulled off his scratched, black fiberglass helmet. There, protruding from the left side of his headgear was a broken-off, pointed end of that black bull's horn.

Now, Don and I have visited since this humiliating mauling he endured on this nearly deserted African road. He never mentioned anything about training to become a Matador to settle the score. Obviously he knows that it is only he and I who are aware of this unfortunate episode.

It's understandable he would never reveal to his northern friends the extent of embarrassment he suffered in his agony of defeat. What kind of a friend would I be to mention this thrashing he received from a battering by a bull?

I photographed a termite mound and myself knowing that I was being watched from the fortified village in the background.

XXV

THE MONEY CHANGER
3-1/2 Degrees North – 24 Degrees East

While riding the wandering, twisting track through the dense jungles of Zaire, I pulled over to the side of the trail and stopped when I saw a line of natives approaching. I dismounted my bike with my camera hanging loosely around my neck. Even though I was alone, I had no fear of regular natives or pygmies. When these tribesmen came past the leaves, that were partially blocking my view, they afforded me a sight that was something I had never seen before in person or in a picture.

Meeting me face to face on this narrow jungle trail were twenty extremely primitive hunters. Walking in single file, each held two weapons. This was one of the most primitive, fierce bands of hard faced Homosapiens that may still be in existence.

I kept my hands out in front of me in plain sight, stayed relaxed and didn't make any real eye contact. They were all about the same size, maybe five foot four, and each wearing animal skins over their lower lean bodies.

I've been in many native villages along rivers and deep in jungles and have never seen evidence of people resembling these. They carried no supplies, not even a water pouch, only a little jungle Tic Tic deer swinging feet up on a pole between the last two of these fierce jungle hunters.

There was no "have a nice day" stuff, as they passed within three or four feet of me. They may not have known how to communicate with others. They only stared at me as if I were another primate of whom they

150

should be apprehensive and attack if provoked. They never saw my bike, as they never took their eyes off my face.

This leaves me pondering where these men fit into the scheme of things. Have they been isolated deep in the jungle for thousands of years, evolving into another sub race?

Another thought: These men, too, are God's creation, and I mean no disrespect in this analogy of mammals. In every isolated village that I have been through, if there are goats, each of them looks alike. If there are dogs, they also appear as brothers. The reason for this is generations of inbreeding. Thus, men too, looked as if they had come from the same strain.

Men cannot roam and hunt indefinitely. From my short encounter with the hunting party that day, I truly believe there are primitive human societies living a nearly savage existence in the deep jungles of Zaire.

I didn't restart my engine until they were beyond the range of its sound. The hard, fierce looks on their faces I will long remember, and my sincere hope is that they always have good hunting and peaceable nights to rest.

I was back to the fascination of the jungle trail and enjoying the unison of bike and rider. Plenty of gasoline in the tank, my canteen nearly full and a sack of raisins and nuts in my pocket gave me a secure feeling about my world. It was a world that was only ten feet wide, ten or fifteen feet in height and a couple hundred feet long. My world may have been small, but it was at peace and embellished with the low tone of my bike's engine, carrying me through the life I love, a life that is challenging; and there in Zaire, always into the unknown.

Though the equatorial sun was unable to shine past the leaves of tree or vine, it cast a lime green glow. The sun's rays were diffused through the millions of leaves, giving a brilliant shadowless view of all within the trail walls.

As the arched trail meandered its way down one of nature's natural hallways, bypassing the jungle's huge trees, finding the path of least resistance it came to an abrupt stop. There, next to a river, a path to the left went up a rather steep bank onto an old railroad tressel. It had been built by the Belgians and left as a better way to cross the stream.

It was a piece of cake riding the railroad ties across, then off and descending the other side. In less than a mile I rode into the back side of an old Western type town.

I greatly enjoyed the jungle, but it was also satisfying to be out, free from the close confinement, and into an area where people should prevail. I had ridden by myself all day and hadn't seen any persons but the twenty primeval hunters with whom I had shared no kinship.

In this city, built before the turn of the century and abandoned after World War II by the Europeans, (as were other cities), the street was broad and lined with tall heavily foliated trees. No vehicles or people were in sight. There was a general store with the front open and a long wooden canopy covering the sidewalk to the street.

It would be nice to stop and buy something just for the experience, but the King Fish with his fiendish comrades had absconded our spending money.

Now the only way to obtain legitimate currency was in the major cities in the south region of Zaire, so I was forced to become a crook and find the illegal moneychanger. The sooner the better, for if there were a soldier or a government official, he would soon be watching me.

When Willy Sutton, one of America's most successful con artists and bank robbers, was asked why he robbed banks, his answer was quick and simple, "That's where the money is."

As I was riding slowly down this wide and fully shadowed street, I never thought of Willy Sutton. However, I was thinking that a bank is the first place to get information as to where the money is.

I've traveled Third World countries enough times to know that even if a bank is closed and boarded up, there is a good chance a small back door will be left unlocked for people, such as myself, with a financial need. The place would be manned by an opportunist.

I saw the bank located back from the street with a round parking area in front. Riding past, I swung around and parked in the shade about a half block beyond the bank. I removed my Belstaff jacket and helmet, scooting them under my bike. Walking back, I crossed the street before reaching the bank and walked around behind the building. There was the back door, left ajar. I reached down, opening the door, and walked in. Across the room sat two men behind desks.

I took out my American Express travelers' checks, holding them up for them to view and told them, "I would like to exchange some money."

No one answered, but the one farthest away got up to leave, walking past me without looking toward me at all. He said two words as he passed, "The Greek."

He kept going, exiting from the one and only door available. I put my American Express folder away and in a couple of minutes I too left, using the door and walked toward the street. I turned left away from my bike in the direction where the business buildings were located. As I walked along the sidewalk, I caught up with the man from the bank.

He was just standing there looking across the street. Neither one of us made signals of any kind, but I knew the building he was looking at was where the illegal moneychanger was located, and I also knew the moneychanger was known as The Greek. I also realized I would need to use extreme caution and remain secretive.

In all of my life, the only laws I've ever broken were traffic laws. I could write a few hair-raising stories on that alone. And I do have to admit I stole more than one kiss, but now within the last week, I'd become a criminal, forced to do so by circumstances. I had crossed illegally back and forth between the Republic of Central Africa and Zaire, as if it were the Iowa and Illinois border crossing. I had taken part in commandeering a barge without the owner's consent, and now I knew the location and had become involved with the black market money changer, which is a very serious crime. Now, because the King Fish had put us into this situation, money, or the obtaining of it, had become a necessary evil.

There was no need to rush, as it was better to sit down now in a place that was out of the way, just to see who was on the street. It was peaceful just sitting under the tropical shade tree looking the situation over to see if anyone was watching me. The only activity involved two local women returning from the town well heavily laden gourds of water balanced on their heads.

I was anxious, however, to meet the moneychanger, possibly not only for the spendable money, but to meet an honest man. It is my opinion that the black market is the near value of money. It's the government bankers who would run the printing presses throughout the night to trade a person out of his hard currency.

In a few minutes I got up, crossed the street, then turned right, going until I reached the building pointed out by the nod of the opportunist. The building was red brick, very plain, no windows on the first floor and just a common wooden door facing the sidewalk. Arriving at the entryway, I reached down, turned the knob, and pushed open the door into a waiting room. I closed the door behind me as I entered. There were two wooden chairs and another door with a transom above.

Using my knuckles on the inner door, I knocked four or five times and stepped back a couple of feet. In just a minute or two, the door opened and a tall black man stood in the doorway looking at me in total silence.

I asked to see The Greek. Again, without speaking, he closed the door. If the truth were known, the word Greek was probably the only common word we had in our two languages.

I stood in the waiting room a few minutes more, leaning against the wall, with the transom letting in the only light. Before long the door opened wide with an invitation to enter.

There, sitting behind the desk, was a white man in his forties, light hair, maybe a bit overweight, and an apparently pleasant attitude.

"Sit down," he told me, making a gesture with his hand. He asked, "How are things on the other side of the river?"

I always try to maintain a neutral facial expression during a conference. But when he asked me, how things were on the other side of the river, he was either guessing and watching my face for an answer, or he may have been the last white man in town and feeling insecure. In speculation, I wondered if the latter were true, and, in his insecurity, he employed an observer to look out of his upstairs windows. He may have already known I had come in from the backside of this community.

"All right, I think," I told him. Much later though, I remembered the Irish couple who operated the General Store across the river in Bangasoo. It was easy to see they were in fear for their lives. This man may have been in the same situation. In our visit that followed, he told me of owning a plantation in the Republic of Central Africa and some day wishing to return.

Hypothetically, if the Greek and the Indian Geronimo were to have met and had a heart to heart visit, Geronimo would tell him of his desires and plans to return to his land in Arizona. Likewise, the Greek would tell his similar ambitions to return to his land in Republic of Central Africa. If later in heaven they meet by chance and continue their conversation, the Greek would say, "Geronimo, did you ever return to your land in Arizona?"

"No," he would answer, "the white man incarcerated me. Did you, Mr. Greek, return to your land in the Republic of Central Africa?" "No," he would answer, "the black man incarcerated me."

When our conversation had reached a point where there was no more information being exchanged, the tone of the Greek's voice changed abruptly and likewise his dialogue. Although polite and courteous, he was deliberate and firm. "I've never seen you before," he told me, "and I'll never see you again; but if our paths ever cross, I'll swear it's the first time I ever saw you. How much money do you want?"

Our paths never again crossed.

XXVI

CURTAINS OF MANY COLORS
3–1/2 Degrees North – 24 Degrees East

Occasionally it was impossible to find a clearing, and we were forced to camp on the trail. One night in particular, we set up camp in the trail, but as close to the side as possible so natives could pass by during the night. To protect our tents and ourselves within, we cut brush, stacking it in piles at each end of our camp.

During the night I heard women talking and getting closer. When they walked into the brush, all was quiet for awhile. Later, as I was watching out of the mosquito-netting window, I saw the reflections of a half-dozen spears being held by natives escorting the women through our camp.

On another night, while still in the swamps, there were so many floating bamboo shafts that we set up our tents over the water of the swamp. The surface was rather smooth as most of the bamboo was lying parallel. However, we could look down between the bamboo trunks and see the motionless black water.

In the early morning light I rolled up my tent and sleeping gear before anyone was up to give me some time for a walk into the jungle swamp. There was a path to follow over the fallen bamboo trunks. I could hear a waterfall so I kept going deeper into the swamp until there was a slight incline and I was out of the swamp and on dry land.

From that point and onward I not only enjoyed the sounds of the jungle but also witnessed the most beautiful of all jungle scenes. Inasmuch as the steam of the Jungle's vaporizing moisture was rising from the surface and foliage, a spectacular display was forming.

The rays of the early morning sun pushed through the moisture-laden air making it appear as moving curtains of many colors.

With the sound of tumbling waters and the angled rays of the sun creating a full spectrum of colors, using high jungle trees on the far side of the clearing as a background, I leaned against a large log to absorb a never-to-be-forgotten moment of tranquillity. The vapors moved as the early morning temperature changed, and the sun slowly rose above the timber's highest growth revealing Mother Nature's three-dimensional curtain of pastel shades.

As I was enjoying my time of total enthrallment and mesmerization in that unspoiled environment, I was informed of my transgression into a monkey kingdom. The informer was King Boisterous himself. A dominant male monkey from high above in the trees challenged me to the old game of Find the Monkey.

Now I've been involved in this contest before, and every time, the monkey makes a monkey out of me. This time I know I can locate the blatantly brash miniature baboon. It isn't that I know I can, but rather that I know I can't resist, because I'm an addict. I'm hooked. I'm a monkey junkie with the endeavor to find, hidden in the tree, the relentlessly chattering primeval primate that may be pointing his finger, screeching in Monkey Tongue, "You didn't descend from me!"

Sitting on that log, I was engrossed in the challenge, in the sound and unique beauty of the moment, when either the sound of footsteps or a sixth sense caused me to look up the trail. Coming toward and walking on by me was a pleasantly attractive native woman carrying on her head a large gourd of water.

My time was spent, and not having marked my trail as I entered, I decided to return before becoming irrevocably lost. The tumbling water went unseen, and the King of the Monkey Tribe again prevailed.

XXVII

HUMAN SCALP
3–1/2 Degrees North – 24 Degrees East

As the afternoon was advancing to evening during yet another day in Zaire, we stopped and turned right into a small jungle clearing.

Before getting our tents established for a long January summer night, a group of warriors came in for a sign language visit. They didn't look threatening, but the length of their spears and the crossbow the oldest of the troop carried gave an indication their looks could be deceiving.

In addition to the impressive tribal facial marking on their cheeks, they had bones protruding through the lower center of their noses. These nose bones looked like chicken wing bones, the ones with knuckles on each end. They were two or three inches long. But there was no way that I would mention the "C" word while I was near these mild-mannered combatants of that bamboo jungle.

Next to the crossbow, the most impressive thing was the headdress of a spear–carrying, short, strongly built young man. He was wearing on his head what appeared to be a human scalp. It looked to be a scalp from a "scared Indian," long, black hair was held straight up and out by an inch-wide headband decorated with beads.

Tim and this cool warrior with the human scalp were similar in size, short and stocky built men and compatible in spirit, each enjoying clowning around. The warrior never looked at or attempted to try on Tim's black motorcycle helmet, which remained hanging on his bike handlebars. It was Tim who influenced the warrior to remove his human headpiece so that Tim could get the feeling of being a warrior by donning the ferociously wild, longhaired war crown.

The population of lice in the headpiece must have been in the hundreds, but after being exposed to the seldom-bathed, unwashed head of Tim, the lice, that did not reach fresh air, must have suffocated in droves.

After the initial acquaintance period was over, a swap meet commenced featuring our T-shirts for their weapons.

Most of the warriors stayed back, but the curious ones mingled with our fellows. Trading was brisk. Our guys ended up with spears, and Jack Hawthorn traded the chief out of his cross bow in exchange for a padlock.

There were a number of poison arrows traded too. The poison arrows were sheaved six or eight together with the poisonous tip ends encased in cornhusk. The ear of corn had been chiseled out leaving the husk in its normal tube shape holding the tips and protecting the warrior from being scratched and poisoned. I have no idea why our guys wanted the poison arrows except possibly to present as a gift to an adversary, telling them it was a native back scratcher.

XXVIII

CONFRONTATION AT THE CITY WELL
Two Degrees North - 24 Degrees East

Because the post office covered most of a city block, Kissingani must have at one time been a high volume source for postal revenue when the city's name was Stanleyville of the Belgium Congo.

When this nation became Zaire and the city became Kissingani, the post office became a nearly unused government building selling a few stamps and distributing a negligible amount of letters from trays.

Entering the building from the west entrance, I asked at an open window for a General Delivery letter for myself. Again I was disappointed that no letter from my wife and infant daughter Belinda had arrived in time.

Seeing this post office gave me an insight as to the high degree of industrial commercial development that had been achieved during the colonial period of their country.

Why the world is the way it is, no one could possibly explain. One thing is mindfully clear. Everything both physical and mental is in a constant period of adjustment.

We spent but a few short hours in Kissingani. Everyone departed on the road east except Sherm Cooper, Dave and me. The three of us detoured south paralleling the Zaire River, formerly the Congo River, hoping to find the Stanley Falls located close to the Equator, just south of the city.

Traveling at a moderate speed to conserve gasoline, we finally crossed a tributary river bridge and continued riding until reaching Wami Rukula, a town with commercial buildings. Not only were we unable to see the falls or gain knowledge of their location, but in all that distance not a single person was seen. Wami Rukula is not an abandoned jungle town. As we saw it from the road, it was not overgrown returning to nature, but rather, all doors and windows had been boarded over and painted. It appeared that the Europeans had left, hoping to return.

Wasting no time, we turned back, knowing the guys would not stop tonight until ready to camp. Conservation of fuel was the key, and to maintain as good an average speed without stopping was a priority. To obtain the best results and reduce fuel consumption, we cruised at twenty–five miles per hour, and to economize even more, we towed each other until we reached the road going east. Now we were on the same dirt road that our buddies were. If anything went amiss, at least we were where we could be rescued.

In the late afternoon on the equator, the sun dropped rapidly. It seemed a very short time, with the sun to our backs, before darkness overtook us. From then on for a couple of hours we were riding by headlight. By headlight all we could see was what the beam illuminated, not even the villages that we would pass through.

Then, up ahead on the right side was a fire. Our buddies had stopped at villages and were able to barter for a chicken in each of two villages. Since the three of us were two or three hours late, you can guess how much chicken was left for us.

No complaints. For, if there had been a trail and we had been able to locate it, we would have enjoyed the experience of taking a bath in and photographing Stanley Falls. The other guys must have had an interesting afternoon, stopping at native villages to barter for chickens. In addition to their bartering, they picked up two Zairean soldiers in Kissingani, who were walking to their home village which would be a two day walk.

The following day we rode into the town of Bafwaboli, a community located on the Tshopo River's eastern bank. The two soldiers were dropped off at a village south of this town.

Our riders were replenishing our water supply from the town well and waiting around for the rest of us to arrive. That's when one of our new riders of less than two weeks used his camera to photograph a native woman pulling a bucket of water from this well.

That was about the last thing he should have done. Because of sickness and deplorable conditions, picture taking in Zaire is against the law, especially in the middle of a town, at their town well where multitudes gather, and then of a woman working hard to lift her container. That particular action brought threats of repercussion during what had been a peaceable January afternoon.

As word spread throughout the town regarding this unfortunate incident, a crowd began to gather. All faces of this swelling throng were at full moon, quiet, but staring big-eyed toward us.

On their side it was time for a leader, as was evidenced by a runner leaving the growing crowd to bring back their chief before it turned into an angry mob.

A quick decision on our side was that two of our riders would return to the village where we left the two uniformed soldiers just a few minutes before. We would bring the two young military in to help save our necks if the situation became ugly.

Time stood still as the native crowd waited for their chief. No one would wait for our side, however, as two of our riders pounded the native's trail at race-track speed trying to reach the soldiers and return while there was still sanity at the well.

Two of the town's young men wanted the film. The perpetrator removed the film and handed it to them unrolled. It was then that the situation reached a higher level of intensity. Looking at the sun darkened roll of 35-mm film freshly taken from his camera, the men tried vainly to locate the woman's image on the film. The two men, thinking they had been tricked when no pictures were visible, started to turn violent and excited the crowd.

The chief arrived and took control, reviewing what had transpired. The wise one of Bafawboli concluded, after seeing that the woman was clothed, had no goiter and wasn't a leper, no harm had been done. The chief turned and left as most of the gathering crowd did likewise. However, the one who thought he had been tricked turned and grabbed Bill Record by his shirt. It was Bill who had been negotiating with the chief. Bill, having his shirt held by two hands, drove his own arms up between the Zairian's arms, breaking the hold on his shirt. Then, with a short punch of his clenched fist, Bill inflicted some embarrassing pain to the Zairian's nose area.

Word had been spread among us Afro Trek riders that if anything happened, not to get into a fight but to leave on our own and meet at the first jungle clearing east of the town. The two riders carrying our soldier friends arrived just as we were leaving. They made a one–hundred–eighty degree turn, taking the soldiers to their home village for the second time within an hour.

With the crowd mostly dispersed, our riders got away without a scratch. The only physical injury was to the native who got a fist in the face. After the dust settled and days passed, he may have been thought of as a goat, but I'd rather believe he was admired by his peers as a man who stood up for what he thought was degrading to one of his people.

XXIX

THE STRANGEST OF BIRDS
2 Degrees North – 27 Degrees East

Just a few miles east of Bafwabol on the left side of the dirt track was a clearing. This became our temporary campsight until we were reorganized and all riders were accounted for.

This clearing was a large open area, possibly two or three acres, surrounded by ten story high trees, curtained with the perennial climbing, hanging vines.

In the early evening light something caused me to look up. It may have been the bird's scream, but whatever it was, I looked up. I saw, by far, the strangest bird I had ever seen. It looked to be the prehistoric Terradaityl, flying just above the treetops east to west. The wing spread was approximately five feet.

As we rode east a few days later, the elevation increased as we left the jungles and we were entering an area of interesting rolling hills. The narrow jungle track became a velvet smooth dirt road. The ground cover was sparse and the trees were just moderate sized and leafed enough to keep the ground shaded. In spite of this pleasant mild climate, we saw no evidence of human inhabitance.

In the jungles of Africa the natives sustain attacks from aggressive warring tribes if they have some warning. For untold generations the people of the rain forest have survived the violence of the raiders by concealing themselves in the thick, impenetrable vines or submerging from sight in the bamboo swamps.

In years past defenseless tribes lived within these hills herding and tending cattle. Unable to protect themselves from tribal war parties, these people were killed or driven into obscurity. The only evidence of a past civilization was small herds of wild cattle.

In racing competition, I can accelerate to the maximum and blast through turns. But I came to view Africa and not to miss anything within sight. Again, it paid off. With the afternoon sun to my back, I was crowning a rounding hill in a southeasterly direction when the road bent left after the high point. On the slight descent in an open area of the trees to my left was again this bird that was the strangest I had ever seen. He was attempting to land.

I saw him before his eyes detected me. His feet were already running hard as he touched the ground. When he heard the low tone of the engine, he turned his head. Unlike most birds, his head was like that of a horse with eyes positioned in a similar location. When he looked, he turned his head entirely over his shoulder, completely facing toward me. Startled by such close proximity, he wanted to flee by running, flapping and flying.

I slowed even more, hoping this very large bird would stop. Rather than stopping, he panicked, trying to get further away. I'm sure he wanted to take off flying but he just couldn't. Again, he turned his head, by now nearly over his back, facing toward me with his huge head, accentuated by those eyes that faced forward, looking straight at me.

He kept running as fast as possible, keeping balanced with that five-foot wing spread. I don't believe any bird would fly to exhaustion. However, its intelligence may have been so low it may not have had brain power enough to gear itself from landing to taking off. In its fleeing panic, the bird in it's clumsiness took the path of least resistance, downhill, off to the left.

That was a twice in a lifetime gratification, seeing this, to me, the strangest of all birds.

XXX

THE ANT WAR
2 Degrees North – 27 Degrees East

I had never seen an ant war, but I became a free–lance photographer and first-hand witness to a deadly battle between the thieving small red ants and the defenders.

The defenders were a larger black ant called the African Driver Ants. People without medical equipment use them in lieu of stitches to close wounds. The way this is done is by holding the ant close to the puckered cut skin. The ants will bite down, but because of a human's thick skin, they can not bite through, holding on until they die.

So it was on this sunny afternoon riding the smooth, dry jungle trail that I saw across the trail in front of me a wide red "S."

Stopping my bike, I walked up close, seeing the half bodies of thousands of red ants. They formed a letter "S," making a path for the escape of yet thousands more red ants trying to flee with the stolen loot. The loot was tiny white rice–shaped eggs being plundered from the sub–surfaced black ant colony.

As thick as the "S" was and as small as the half bodies were, the battle must have been raging for hours and seemingly with an inexhaustible reserve of ants to do combat.

The battle line was evenly spaced, with no massive concentration at any one location. Rather, the black ants were stationed approximately every half-inch, fighting frantically as the continuous mass of red ants just kept coming, carrying their miniature contraband.

In an ant war the black ants' jaws completely close as they cut the enemy's body in two. Thus they can bite over and over again. Each black ant stands his ground, only moving from side to side killing the egg-carrying red ants as they attempt to pass. Each black ant must have killed an uncountable number of the thieving red enemy by biting into them.

I had to get down close to see. Running through the half bodies were masses of red ants. They were recovering the eggs dropped by the dead ants, carrying them on as in a relay only to be killed and again dropping the loot. Then the loot would be recovered by another ant, it being killed, and the process being repeated over and over again. The red ants' duration in the fight was that of the suicidal Kamikaze pilot, while the larger black ant must have stood his ground and fought, possibly, for hours.

There probably has never been a truly neutral observer during a war. I was no exception, for I have no use for a thief. It is my belief that they are one of the lower forms of life. On the other hand, a soldier who will stand his ground and fight for his own should be held in the highest esteem.

How could it be? Me, with my supportive thoughts and without provocation being attacked by those vice-jawed black warriors?

I ran back to my bike, hung my camera on the handlebars, jerked off my boots, pulled off my pants and started taking hold of the black ants' bodies with their legs flogging. It may have hurt them more than me, but they at least have returned to dust. I still carry their scars.

While performing my white-legged dance, I noticed the local natives were watching the show. If they enjoyed my matinee performance, they could have at least thrown coins; and if not, they could have thrown fruit. I always relish an afternoon snack.

XXXI

NIA NIA
2 Degrees North – 28 Degrees East

Whether there was a town of Nia Nia, I couldn't say, but there is a triangle shaped intersection in the middle of where a town could have been.

As we approached the intersection from the west, we passed a row of unused cement granaries. The granaries were the first indication of a hard fought conflict during their war. I only saw one side of the building, but that side was covered with a multitude of potholes from hundreds of rounds of small arms fire.

Entering the triangle intersection, we turned toward the south, slowed down and parked. After parking our bikes in a row, we left to examine the field of battle. At one time this was a pleasant setting with shade trees and shrubbery.

Nia Nia was not unlike other jungle stops. When we approached and shut off the engines of our quiet, deep-toned Hondas, the intersection was vacant.

In the intersection was a "knocked out" light military tank. It had been hit hard by cannon fire but never burned. We climbed on its top and inspected the inside of the tank but were unable to see much.

At the west inside point of the intersection was a concrete monument covering the grave of Lt. Sylvester of the British Army. The monument was in two tiers with a short, thick Christian cross bearing the lieutenant's name at the base.

On the far east side was an old, country, one–room gasoline station. The gasoline company's logo remained in the front of the station. Abandoned and very dingy was the Shell Oil Company's scalloped shaped sign. This sign would have been manufactured stateside with pride, brought nearly halfway around the world for a growing nation to use. Now, as was most of Zaire, it was forgotten and deteriorating.

On returning to our motorcycles, we found a row of men, twelve or fifteen of them, standing shoulder to shoulder facing us and standing just behind our bikes.

Photography was illegal in Zaire because of the deplorable conditions; however, I still wanted to take more shots. We all started our engines with these native men standing behind our bikes and rode off, except myself. I watched the natives' faces. They all turned, watching the motorcycles disappearing, giving me time to shoot three quick pictures. I got shots of the Shell gas station, the army tank and Lieutenant Sylvester's monument, getting away from them without conflict.

The Belgium military tank is apparent in the center of the picture. In the right foreground is the grave of Lt. Sylvester, an Englishman.

XXXII

OKAPI, GIRAFFE FROM THE PAST
2 Degrees North – 27 Degrees East

We stopped near a building that sported a painting of an Okapi on the wall facing the roadway. We found a person living nearby who agreed to show us an Okapi, one of the most rare of larger animals.

He took us past a fence and north up a cool green valley. Standing there were three of these relatives of the giraffe, lazily wrapping their tongues around tree leaves, munching the afternoon away. Unlike the giraffe who looks like he was put together by a city planning committee, the Okapi is built more to proportion. With a long neck and horns located farther down the scull than a giraffe, their forelegs are more similar in length to the hind legs. The body is slim in stature and stands at least five and one-half foot at the shoulder.

They look to be nearly shiny black with white stripes running horizontally on their rumps and upper front legs. The lower legs are black and white. The front kneecaps look like a bull's eye, black spot in the middle, a white circle and another black ring with two black stripes going down either side of their white background, giving them the most colorful and attractive front lower limbs imaginable.

This local fellow, who has to some extent tamed these three Okapis, told of twenty–six Okapis in this valley and at least six more in another valley in the lower region west of the Virunda Mountains.

British team capture first pictures of Africa's 'Unicorn'
was the Yahoo News headline, 9/11/08, referring to the Okapi

At one time this mysterious animal was thought to be a mythological unicorn. The Zoological Society of London claims to have taken the first photo ever of the Okapi in the wild using a camera trap. Yet in January 1975 I took this photo of the Okapi and 2 more. I used a 55mm with a 3X telephoto lens.

XXXIII

ILLEGAL IVORY AND THE POACHER
1 Degree North – 29 Degrees East

Mambasa is a sparsely inhabited city in eastern Zaire. It lies in the rolling hills above the Epulu River's south bank. Even though it was midday in this step country's rather large town, we saw no more than a half dozen people. The first was attending a gasoline station with a huge truck parking area. We may have been his only customer that day as vehicles were just non–existent.

At the hotel, which was just up the street a half mile from the gasoline station, we stopped to have refreshments and escape from the bright noontime sun. The waiter was a clean-cut fellow wearing black pants and a long sleeved white shirt and a vest. He and the large gasoline station were reminders of a more prosperous time.

The third person was an attractive American lady with blonde hair in her late twenties. She was sitting at a table just letting time pass. I joined her for a visit. In our conversation I got the feeling she was returning to the people she "missed" from her Peace Corp days and was contemplating staying to live with them.

The fourth individual was an opportunist who dealt in illegal ivory. We followed this guy into a residential district where we parked and left our bikes. There were no streets over this low, rolling hill; there were just rows and rows of round adobe and straw houses. After walking nearly a quarter of a mile through a walking alley, this fellow stopped at one of the round adobe houses, rapped on the door, then went inside.

The mud-brick house consisted of two rooms. The fellow evidently lived in one room. The other was full of

172

art crafts. Reasoning tells me the place was so concealed because he was selling illegally obtained ivory.

There must have been between fifty and one hundred long, crescent-shaped tusks from now decomposed bodies left in eastern Zaire bush country.

One of the most notable carvings was from a long tusk, and depicted a twenty-horse hitch on a covered cargo wagon. It brought back memories of the twenty-mule-team hitch pulling wagons loaded with borax from quarries in the California/Nevada desert as shown on black and white television's "Death Valley Days."

I felt very out of place. However, I did purchase the cheapest thing he had to show my contempt, four ivory pickle forks, then departed.

Outside, a few houses away, were a pair of three–year–old twin children and their mother. One was busy pounding grain into powder. He was using an instrument shaped like a ball bat and vertically pounding straight down onto the top of a hard wood concaved stump.

"That would make a great picture," I thought. So I gave the mother some money and showed her my camera. About then a big authoritarian looking guy came from between two houses. The lady never looked up but slowly shook her head. I put my camera away easily as he passed. The twin's mother came over to me and from her tight little brown hand dropped the money I had given her into my hand. It was evident she wanted no problems with the poachers.

XXXIV

RODEO IN THE ZAIREAN JUNGLE
1 Degree North – 29 Degrees East

After leaving Mambasa, we followed the dirt road leading east through many very primitive villages. It was not unusual for the natives to come running out to the road, waving and cheering as we passed. Some would bend over to look up at my face because of my duck-billed helmet. It was great fun to cheer while waving back to these friendly people. Pygmies could also be seen along the roads; however, their villages were hidden deep in the bush.

The trails that we traveled could not be considered the runway for a fashion show, but some of the apparel we observed, or the lack thereof, had a tendency to generate some extra attention. It was difficult to keep expressions in check as my facial muscles were stretched to their limits while I tried to refrain from grinning.

For example, one morning a few of the ladies were out for a walk. The apparel of the day for two of the well-built ones was banana leaves. Now these banana leaves were placed around the waist and tied with more leaves. The leaves hanging from the waist covered what the ladies did not want to show. As they walked along the trail, time and temperature took their toll and had a tendency to dry the banana leaf skirts. With the rhythmic oscillation of the feminine extremities, the leaves began to fall. By the time we rode past, autumn had already arrived. The leaves had long departed, leaving in full view the southern exposure.

If this had been a fashion show, the winners with a perfect ten would have been a pair of tiny Pygmy people. This couple was in formal attire. He was wearing a black tuxedo, his lovely lady, a white, full-length evening gown; they were dressed as if preparing to attend a presidential ball. Rather than being in an eloquent neighborhood with fine homes, they were at the edge of town walking in the grass next to the dirt road.

Later that same evening we took advantage of a rare jungle clearing to set up camp early. With a couple of hours to waste before dark when we would have our soy meat and coffee, we riders put on a motorcycle thrill show for the local natives.

We performed the usual dance, riding wheelies, turning doughnuts, anything we thought we could do better than the next guy. Each time a rider completed one of his antics, I would lead the native crowd in cheers and heavy applause. When the stunt show was completed, the natives kept up the spirit by clapping and shouting with approval.

One of the spectators, a Pygmy woman standing near the edge of the clearing and watching, was as unclothed as a person could be. For gentlemanly reasons I smiled and waved. When the garmentless-gal-of-the-bush returned my smile, she was self-conscious of her appearance. Raising her hand, she covered her mouth because she had a front tooth missing.

XXXV

TRANSVERSING THE MOUNTAINS
OF EASTERN ZAIRE
1 Degree North – 30 Degrees East to
2 Degrees South – 29 Degrees East

Leaving the sandy road approximately a hundred miles south of Nia Nia, we turned left up a two-track, winding trail over the foothills of Mount Hoye.

After camping for the night, we started out early on foot up the jungle trails of Mt. Hoye's west slope. Employing the guidance of two natives carrying Coleman lanterns, it was our plan to explore the caves deep within this porous mountain. The trail, either by plan or coincidence, passed one of the world's most colorful waterfalls. Dropping a few hundred feet over hundreds of steps, the tumbling waters picked up the brilliant colorations from the mineral stained stone, the shades of green plant life and the sun's reflective effects. The descending water maintained perpetual motion reflecting the waterfall once again in its large bowl–shaped pool at the base of the waterfall.

In addition to receiving such a magnificent view of the falls, I could also stand directly across and watch the falling waters in reverse, picking up the tint of the blue sky in the delightful rippling waters. The world has thousands of magnificent natural scenes, but the grandeur and beauty of moving colors has to be a rarity.

It was evident from the tracks that big, soft-footed animals had been drinking regularly from the colorful rounded pool. The natives soon directed us up a tree-lined, shady animal trail.

After some time the mountainside became steep and treeless with the dirt ending near a flat outcropping of a horizontal plate rock. Following north on the rock ledge, we soon reached a cave opening about the size of a garage door.

The natives went inside, carefully counting their footsteps. It must have been nearly twenty-five paces in the near darkness before one native stopped, pointing down at the level cavern floor. One at a time we stood on the indicated spot to look toward the entrance.

The sight was amazing. From high above the world, all that was visible was an azure sky; however, from that exact spot the blue sky was the likeness of the African continent with the outline formed by the rough interior walls of the cave. In other words, the spectacle was a light blue map of Africa with a near-black, rock outline.

If you have ever been to New York City, you will remember that you can't see New York from New York. You have to cross over to New Jersey, then stop, turn around and look across the river, that is, if you want to see New York. Mt. Hoye is somewhat the same. I saw its beautiful waterfall, walked its paths, explored miles of its caverns, but I never saw the mountain.

Be that as it may, another good walk and we arrived at the entrance to miles of interior, eroded passageways. Our plan was to try the sport of cave exploration. The two natives lit their Coleman lanterns while we put on our jackets. Within minutes after arriving, all of us were in the cavity, high on the mountainside.

Walking single-file in darkness, the only person who could see clearly was the person carrying the lantern. So it was for hours, exploring the miles of caves deep within Mt. Hoye's west slope.

One of the natives who guided us let us know he explored the cave often. However, if he was referring to this cave, what he said was untrue. We were making the only deep footprints in the bat droppings on the cavern floor.

As we descended deeper into the recess of those caves, the floor became slanted at a steep angle. At that time it was no longer a cave but rather a wide, slanting, subterranean slash which went downward to the left. This

177

slash seemed bottomless. If anyone slipped, he would roll downward into the darkness and, doubtless, never be seen again. The sound of descending screams would forever haunt the survivors.

We came to many vertical cracks, the depth of which I have no idea. To transverse these, the man with the longest legs went first. For some semblance of security we would grasp each other, hands to wrist, while making the risky, wide and steep crossings.

Daylight was visible a couple of hours into the subterranean journey. Through one of the cracks we could see blue sky off to the right and high above, a reminder there was another life on the outside.

To see the light of freedom held no reassurance since we were still entrapped within this hazardous, underground environment where only bats and beetles, which survive on bat droppings, exist.

There was no conversation. We were using our entire concentration as we crept along in the darkness of this cavity within Mt. Hoye's porous interior.

Rather than enjoying an adventure of exploring this underground cavern, our exploit this day turned into a chamber of horrors. The tense anxiety from realizing that one of us could become enveloped in eternal darkness was constantly at the forefront of reality.

The long ordeal ended with a glow of the exterior light from beyond the shadowy lantern's yellow reflection on the gray rock ceiling. The ending was solemn. Never again.

Just to the south of the cave's exit were enclaves within the mountain wall. These enclaves were all at the same level on solid rock, but the interior had eroded leaving a hemisphere with a western exposure. I could stand and look outwards thousands of feet above the jungle, and see to the west nothing but multi-colored green, with distances limited only by the jungle's moist haze. Wild animals used these rounded, half–tennis court size recesses for part of their habitat, for the floors were covered with imprints of animal tracks.

We continued walking east along this mountain ridge overlooking the vast treeland with the afternoon's sun reflecting its glow until we saw a well–used animal trail descending through the rain forest.

Taking the last view, looking across thousands of acres of jungle from a high mountain vantage point, we started our long descent. This animal trail must have been well used because it was worn smooth and also wider than most. Like other trails I had been on, it bypassed massive jungle trees, which had large external roots giving the needed extra support. At this higher altitude it was possible to see into the mountainside forest, not only to view its picturesque beauty but also to watch for wild life.

Arriving at the foothills near dusk, we came to a cave having a boulder within the size of a Goodyear Blimp. The tremendous granite rock was water-splattered by sprinklings from the cave's gigantic ceiling. Three or four of our guys were able to scale the granite side of the wet rock to take an icy-cold evening shower.

After a couple more days in the highlands and forest of the Ruwenzori Mountains, we descended into the town of Butembo, still in Zaire. Butembo sits on the temperate foothills, a well laid out and populous community.

Ralph Hurtienne and I stopped to visit their one-room general store, which had a sparse stock of Chinese merchandise. However, the most memorable and shocking sight was in the glass-faced counter.

There, for anyone to see, was a lower human leg bone still locked in a rust-covered set of iron leg shackles. Rather than a total white bashing of slavery, I have read and believe, because of gifts to chiefs and the difficulty of transversing the lands of Africa, the village and/or territorial chiefs were also largely involved in that horrible transgression. Yet today we read of obtaining slaves by trickery or force as a widespread practice in some areas.

When we came out of the general store, a crowd had gathered. Ralph's rear tire was going flat. We changed the inner tube and aired it up with our small hand pump. I was rolling up my tool bag and attempting to put my jacket on as the mass of young men pushed so close it bothered me. I forced my way up. Raising both of my arms, shouting, "Get back, get back."

The curious young men must have thought I was being courteous in welcoming them, for many of them, too, raised up their arms repeating, "Get back, get back," seeming as a gesture of friendship.

The morning of January 16 we crossed the equator just south of Butembo. As our trek continued southward, we passed just west of Lake Edward, paralleling the Great Riff Valley, and on into the Virunga Mountains. Further south lay Lake Kivu. East of there flowed the Kagerar River, the most remote source of the Nile, discovered by Sir Henry Stanley in 1874. Three years earlier and only a few miles south is where Sir Stanley uttered the famous greeting, "Dr. Livingston, I presume."

By mid–afternoon, still on the 16th, we started our descent on the loose surfaced mountain roads. Four of us lined up for a push-start, downhill, dead engine race.

Coasting dead engine became darned exciting and extremely competitive as we descended those twisting, rocky, bumpy mountain roads. There was a lot of passing and repassing as we bid for position, trying to gain an advantage over one another.

The switchback turns became an instant peril when entered at an excessive speed without power to assist in cornering. If one touches the brakes in that situation, the peril compounds instantly. Entering a turn at excessive speed was Jack Hawthorn's near demise. His front tire lost traction, putting him into an involuntary slide. His slide ended abruptly about a hundred feet down the canyon wall.

The only tree near the path of his uncontrollable slide stopped his fall in a heartbeat. Otherwise, he would have disappeared deep into the rocky valley below.

I refrained from taking foolish chances mainly because of remembering my wife's plea as I departed back in the states, "Jerry, be careful." It may have been love or the fact that a good man is hard to find. Whatever the reason, when a choice was offered I heeded her plea.

Jack wasn't penalized his position, but a good half hour was lost using rope and muscle before we lined up for an even restart. With no road signs of upcoming villages, we would flash through in seconds, our bodies flat on the gas tank, toes in and elbows tucked to reduce wind drag.

It wasn't our intention to go recklessly through their little wide spots in the road. We were as surprised as they. But, I can surmise the native translation of their dialect, "What was that?" And as we flashed by, the reply, "What's What?"

Finally we came to a stop on a high ridge overlooking a vast east Zaire savanna. From where I was stopped, I could see for immeasurable miles the light tan grassland. With the help of binoculars it was possible to make out small groups of foraging animals in the afternoon sun.

The road down was typically a rocky, sandy, twisting descent. We soon saw evidence of the natural inhabitants, as partridges scurried from the road. By evening we had made it to the basin below where we rode through a herd of water buffalo. There were three species of antelope, warthogs, two repulsive hyenas; and in the distance there were two huge elephants.

Across the savanna we rode into DesBirungs National Park's hunting lodge of RuWundi. It was nearly dark when we arrived and were told it was too dangerous to sleep in tents because of the big animals coming through. How right the employee was since the lodge was within a short walking distance from a river.

At the lodge there were only two park employees and an American from Minnesota. In a conversation with the Minnesotan, we discovered I had met and visited with his wife and two children on a roadside back in Central Zaire.

In the early morning a large rhinoceros was milling around one of the cabins. Everyone wisely stayed clear, giving him full latitude. From his slow walk, he stopped, raised his tail and discharged his high-pressure, gas-propelled excrements with a force that I'm at a loss to describe. Next his flat-footed, thick-skinned, nearly hairless buddy stopped by for refreshment. Instead of dipping his trunk into the nearby river, he strolled over to the wooden, open-topped people's water tower. He raised up, hanging his trunk over the edge, apparently taking a good drink, thus satisfying his thirst.

Jim Squires and I pause with our rear wheels in the northern hemisphere and our front wheels in the southern.

XXXVI

GOMA, AN OL' FRONTIER TOWN
2 Degrees South – 29 Degrees East

There is a sign at the entrance to Panama's airport. It reads, "Panama, Crossroads of the World - The Intersection of the Universe." Goma, Zaire, has no catchy sign. However, if it did, the sign could read, "Goma, A Big Degree South of the Equator, Intersected by the World's Most Famous (Earthquake) Fault."

Because Goma's mother country had rotted to a standstill, the frontier town had reverted to a quiet community. It was probably supported by the people living along the Virunga Mountain foothills, those people who may live off the faults or Lake Kivu, and those crossing from Rwanda.

It was mid–afternoon when we rode down the main thoroughfare. It was wide and unused. We stopped and parked our bikes in the middle of the smooth street. Dismounting from our bikes, we found it convenient to merely hang our gear over the handlebars and across the seats. Looking down upon us from a second story, wrought iron balcony was a local white businessman who hollered at us in English, "Watch your stuff; it will be stolen."

Unlike a jungle village where a thief would be held down and strangled to death if caught stealing, here the penalty was apparently less formidable or the thieving outlaws were faster on foot.

The first thing that needed my attention after parking was finding a cobbler to replace a heel on my boots. This was the third time I had jerked a heel off in a Third World country, and I knew that to retrieve the heel was essential. For if Goma, Zaire, was like other places

I've been, the people dismantled old shoes for their nails and leather.

Earlier on this trip I stopped the most unique "man in blue," a Tareg, as he walked down the streets of Tamanrassett, Algeria. I showed him my boot with no heel. He was dressed in the traditional blue robe and wore a matching blue turban that, except for a shaded recess from which he observed his world, totally covered his face. He greeted me warmly.

Motioning me to accompany him, we returned north on the main street in Tamanrasset to a narrow arched access on the east side of the street and entered Tamanrasset's Bazaar. There were at least thirty small shops sitting behind a larger arched main entranceway. The Tareg and I walked slowly down the sandy midway, giving me time to absorb what I was seeing.

The Tareg showed me to the last archway on the left. Here I had to step inside out of the sun's vertical rays, pausing to let my eyes adjust to the darkness of the room.

Inside were a barber and his client, both sitting cross-legged in their robes on the dark, sandy floor. One was trying to remain still as the other clipped away most of his remaining hair with scissors. A third man was the shoe cobbler. I walked over, handed him my problem boot and heel, then joined the others sitting on the dirty sand floor. At a workbench not more than a foot tall, he went to work taking out old nails, pounding them straight. Using a dab of glue and recycled nails, my old boot was as good as new within a few minutes.

A couple of years earlier in the high mountains of Costa Rica, Central America, a half world away, I had to jab my foot hard to save my BMW's tires from kicking out on a rocky ox-cart and jeep road. A day or two later with the heel I had retrieved in my pocket, my wife Jo and I arrived in front of a house where my boot could be repaired. This house looked small, three or four rooms; but, by a hundred fold, its setting was the most daring place for human residence I have ever seen. The house was protruding from the canyon wall about twenty feet on a pillar of stone. To leave this house in any other direction, the first step would have been a doozie: hundreds of feet, maybe a thousand or more of the fresh air of the ravine before a person would begin bouncing.

To cross over from the road, one had to step onto a two-foot wide suspension bridge that was cut out along the canyon wall.

Inside this home, which sat like an eagle's nest, was a pleasant Latin American family of four. In their living room the cobbler used a dab of glue and some old, straightened nails to reinstall the heel of my boot.

Goma, Zaire's, shoe cobbler was no different from the other two. Only the location had changed. This craftsman of footwear had taken over the occupancy of an unused house for hogs. His business looked to be slow, but his overhead was virtually nil, and a member of the swine family would not be returning to reclaim the living quarters until the enlightenment of mankind.

It was a pleasure to walk down the sidewalks of Goma. This was the first town since Bangui in the Republic of Central Africa, twenty–five days before, where a person could sit down and eat in a restaurant. The post office was one room and memorable for the postage stamps being sold. These stamps showed the likeness of two great American prizefighters, George Forman and Mohammed Ali, who had fought in the capital city of Kinshasa in the early to mid–seventies.

We camped that night in a lava field west of Goma. The lava had solidified with rounded bubbles all the same height, eight or ten inches and far enough apart that a person could walk.

South of Taylor Reservoir in the Colorado Rockies there is another nearly identical lava field. I saw Harold Daigh of Rollin Hills, California, discover this field when he overshot a gravel-road turn while nearly maxed out on his XL600 Honda. As he flew into the field, everything looked rideable. But with deceleration Harold hunched over the bars, hanging onto his bike like a wild rodeo star trying to retain his hold, finally bringing the hair raising ride to a stop with the wheels lodged within a lava trench. Bill

Wood of the American Motorcycle Association and I tried vainly to stay with the Flying Daigh while riding an off road motorcycle event called the Colorado 500.

Neither Bill nor I could run out to help retrieve Harold or his Honda. It was an effort just to find a place for our feet while trying to walk.

It was such a condition in which we camped near Goma. In the morning I found my plastic tent had attracted a multitude of snails, all sucked tight to the tent's outside smooth surface.

Twenty-one days of witnessing a sampling of the natives' personal lives in Equatorial Africa's Zaire came to an end at the border crossing with Rwanda, located just south of Goma on the shores of Lake Kivu.

On this lake there was a unique phenomenon occurring. During the early morning hours a slight steamy haze lay on the water's surface, intermingling with the light, low, overcast sky. A few hundred yards off shore was a sailboat made from a canoe and having an outrigger.

The boat was floating along at full sail. There was no definition between the hazy mist of the lake's surface and the low white fogginess. It appeared that the vessel was floating through the heavens, riding the white hazy clouds.

Before crossing into the nation of Rwanda in January 1975, there had been approximately six hundred thousand people murdered. This wholesale killing of men, women and children was referred to by the fatalistic name, "The Final Solution." The tribes of the Watusi and the shorter Hutu had been at odds with each other since the fourteenth century.

As I wrote this story during the summer of 1994, another fateful chapter was being recorded in the "Life and Death on Planet Earth." The killing of another half million humans was taking place. This was similar to the previous butchering of innocent natives, only the generation and the losers had been changed. If there is a lesson to be learned, that lesson should have been learned a host of centuries ago.

Leaving the frontier and Zaire behind, we started up a long winding incline away from Lake Kivu. Here we saw for the first time flowers growing next to a home, roads of ample width to accommodate two vehicles meeting and people who looked as though they had a purpose.

Rwanda, the Ozarks of Africa

XXXVII

RWANDA, OZARKS OF AFRICA
2 Degrees South – 29 Degrees East

I came to a stop along a tree-lined road high on the north rim of a valley. Parking my bike on the shady road, I dismounted, and taking my camera with me, walked to the edge of the high rim. Looking nearly straight down a few hundred feet, I saw a small native farmstead, very picturesque on the floor of the valley.

On the far ridge facing me were rows of terraces starting near the valley floor and extending upward in tiers to the crest of the hillsides. These terraces appeared to be the result of years of agriculture and seemed to be from an earlier culture.

After viewing the unusual terraces and taking a few pictures, I returned the camera to its case and zipped it shut. I turned around, returning to my parked bike.

My motorcycle was parked in the shade and because I was returning from very bright sunshine, I didn't immediately notice a Watusi native standing to the left side of my bike. There wasn't a noticeable expression, neither good nor bad. Rather, he was just looking straight into my face.

I nodded and spoke without receiving any recognizable acknowledgment. As he kept staring at my face, I soon got an uneasy feeling since there were only the two of us in this isolated place. He was standing rather close to me. Therefore, instead of mounting from the proper side, which would have me turning my back to him, I mounted from the right-hand side. I started my bike and bid him what I thought was a farewell.

I clicked my bike into low gear, riding away smoothly. He too, must have gotten in gear, for when I accelerated away, he remained right beside me, not breaking his stare. I went to second gear and noticeably increased my speed. His speed likewise increased.

Now, trying to outrun this speedy Watusi didn't worry me, even though unfortunately, I have thought I had the greatest speed and been proven wrong in the past. In an all out race of man against machine, I was sure he wasn't carrying that much gas, and I still had three more gears to go.

It would have been interesting to see how fast and long he could run, but I was concerned that he would grab my bike or me. I shifted gears and gave my machine more throttle. I have noting but admiration for a man who could challenge me and run my bike well up into third gear.

Riding through Rwanda may have been similar to a ride through the Ozark Mountains. All the roads were winding over or around the rolling hills and the surface was a sandy loam.

It was on a main road that was being repaired by one of the Chinese road crews that we met China's version of a bad attitude. When the driver of a large road grader saw us approaching, as he was doing a fine job of finishing, he stopped his smoothing operation and blocked us from passing.

There was no method of passing with the road grader crosswise, so rather than getting into a confrontation, we turned back and found a place to camp out of sight, for it was already time to let the bikes rest for the night.

The three days and two nights required to cross this little country were tranquilizingly pleasant. We camped on farms where local farmers would come out and spend time with us. During drive time the terrain was either timber-covered hills, or small farms on hilltop plateaus or along rolling hillsides.

It wasn't unusual to pass through a village and notice the lack of population or to see a woman walking on the road smoking a pipe.

Externally Rwanda was a nation of peace and tranquility, but internally there must be a terrible hate between the tribes.

Looking down upon a native farmstead, I could see the terraced fields.

XXXVIII

BAYONETS AND CHAMBERED ROUNDS
1 Degree South – 34 Degrees East

The trails of the Serengeti have existed as long as animals have roamed the plains. The roaming animals were the architects of the twisting paths, never using T corners or tight turns, but a winding blend of soil and scenery. At third and fourth gear speeds on the four stroke, we settled into a rhythmic search of never-ending trails, riding firmly in the saddle, loose on the bars, with an occasional brush of a pucker bush. The motorcycle turned motion into music.

I rode alone in the ecstatic freedom of a wonderland near Lake Victoria in the northern Serengeti, not realizing we would be transformed from adventurers to intruders and subjected to bayonets and chambered rounds before the morning sun would rise.

When I left the trails to refuel, I talked Jack Hawthorn and Dick Bettencourt into leaving the pleasures of the dust and bumps of the gravel-road riding to join me on the fast tracks of the wildebeest. Away we went with Hawthorn in the lead. The race was on to see who would show the other his backside. Now Dick Bettencourt's greatest desire has never been to be number two, and Hawthorn wasn't about to back off. Wheel to wheel, chasing through the winding turns, our temptation to eat from the forbidden fruit was overwhelming.

We've all been tempted to take a bite, but Dick took the big one – right through a pucker bush. The cymbals rang, the drums rolled, the pinnacle was reached as wheel and stump united to form the concert's climactic conclusion. The rider lay prone. The fat lady never sang.

There would be no joy in Mudville tonight.

Waiting for Afro Annie, our support truck, I covered Dick with my space blanker, silver side up, trying to keep the sun's rays away from him. He sat up and we stabilized his arm to help keep his broken shoulder bone from doing its thing.

It wasn't long until Dick and his Honda were loaded on board and heading to a Red Cross we saw marked on the Michlen's map. The town of Musoma was three or four hours' ride away and on Lake Victoria.

Three of us, Jack Hawthorn, Don Murk and I, rode ahead. It was evening and nearly dark as we rode into town. Main Street was like an old, turn-of-the-century, Midwestern borough, no doubt built by the Europeans many years ago. The wooden sidewalks were covered with wooden canopies attached to store fronts. The streetlights were few and very dim, and we saw no one as we rode through. The electricity source was from a few blocks back and powered by a yellow Caterpillar diesel turning a large generator.

The hospital, which looked much like a barracks, was easy to find, just east to the end of main street, turn right into the drive, then left. Parking our bikes, we walked south to an entranceway where an outside light was shining. I was looking in through the window of the locked main entrance door, discovering this hospital was like the one in Tamanrasset, empty and no longer in use.

As I stepped back from the window, a native warrior walked up. He was one of the tallest men I've ever seen. All he was wearing was an animal skin, for modesty sake only. His head and facial features were difficult to see because his height put his face in the shadow from the hooded light fixture. His left hand was free, but in his right hand he held a very long bow and five or six arrows. He may have been watching us from the darkness, for when I tried the door and was looking through its window, he came forward to help me make a decision. Don't try entering.

Jack, with his limited use of three languages, tried every word to describe our plight of needing a physician. When the warrior left, we felt relieved that help was coming to set Bettencourt's broken shoulder. A half-hour passed before Bill Record arrived. Dick and Sherm Cooper were back at Afro Annie in the parking lot.

We were visiting in the glow of the light bulb above us as we awaited the imminent arrival of the doctor. Three were sitting on the cement steps looking out. I was standing back a short distance looking in, when from my left side vision, I saw the three golden colored bayonets protruding past the corner of the building. I did not move or look, just told the guys that there were bayonets coming around the edge of the building.

Record said, "Don't anyone move quickly, but keep talking."

I was standing with my back to the darkness knowing something, over which I had no control, was about to happen. I would just be a recipient.

Softly in the muscle on the right side of my back, just above the belt, I could feel the tip of a bayonet. I could tell by the faces of my buddies facing me that we were surrounded, as each man was looking at something different. I was hoping that whoever they were, they already had our two men at the support truck. At any kind of surprise, a jumpy soldier could squeeze off a round and all hell could break loose, making for lonesome girlfriends and sad widows back home.

An officer spoke; no one answered. Again he spoke, this time in English. He wanted our passports. Any conversation is better than silence. In silent darkness monsters build inside the minds of men.

He was told of our injured man in the truck while he was looking at our passports. After looking through each one, he put them into his uniform jacket pocket.

After visiting with his men, the officer left and didn't return for a half-hour. In the meantime we fellows stayed as we were, but we went back to visiting while a dozen soldiers kept their golden bayonet rifles trained at our largest target area.

We were marched out to our bikes and told to start them and ride in a close group. We followed running soldiers while other soldiers running on each side and behind kept their bayoneted guns leveled toward us.

We were taken north toward the lake, finally up a long hill, and then to the left into a Tanzaniaean army camp. The soldiers maintained a fast run without ever breaking stride and seemed to be a polished outfit far superior to the army of Nicaragua who had me interned two years before.

Our bikes were parked under a light within a fenced area. All of us were taken inside an interrogation room. The floor was on two levels with a low railing between. We were on the lower level and the officer and some of his men were on the higher floor. No one ever removed his finger from the triggers.

We were not yelled at, pushed or intimidated other than by the constant readiness of their weapons. However, Bettencourt was shown no mercy or consideration. Inside he stood motionless, using his good arm to hold himself in such a way as to keep the fractured bones from gritting together. (A few years later, Sherm Cooper, Bettencourt and I were eating together at a banquet in Houston. Bettencourt told us he had no memory of that night.)

Where we stopped when coming in is where we remained standing until well after midnight. The same officer that was in charge when we were taken into custody didn't turn us over to higher officials but retained authority over us.

We faced the banister and the soldiers. The interrogation commenced by using questions about country, nations, and families, including information of both mother and father in detail such as their place of birth, where they live and have lived. It was important to be consistent with each answer, as we would be drilled over and over again. Thinking back, we must have sounded like basketball teams using names like Boston, Iowa, Washington, Minnesota. The only personal good of this was recalling, with visual remembrance, my loving parents.

The officer, through hours of inquiry, referring to our passports, making notations on form, remained sharp and alert. His men, too, were well–disciplined, hardly moving with rifles at the ready.

Before each soldier left, his gun was pointed toward the ceiling and the breach was cleared by extracting the cartridge, then clicking off the firing pin.

Taking their place were six riflemen from some type of elite guard. Rather than wearing tans, they wore olive pants and sweaters with a black leather patch atop their shoulders. They, too, pointed their rifles toward the ceiling, shoving a cartridge into the chamber, then bringing the rifle down ready to fire. This unit was neat in appearance. Their uniforms fit properly and their weapons were polished. But one at least was lacking in personal discipline during the wee hours of the morning. With us being on the lower level and them on the higher floor level, it was easy to notice one was a trimly built woman with a desire for her own excitement. The men in proper military fashion kept both hands on their weapons. But she found a better way, and it was much less boring. She let the rifle stock rest on her thigh, leaving her left hand free to play the organs.

By candlelight and soft music, this could have lead to a romantic encounter. She moved over to a second organ that was more in tune, giving me a feeling she might trigger the wrong finger and end up shooting the pigeons off the roof. If feathers started flying, this cowboy was ready to dive under the welcome mat.

Before the fun ended, the outside door behind us opened. Again it was regular army soldiers with fixed bayonets motioning us outside and directing our leg–weary group to start walking away from the dim yard light, where our bikes were parked, and into the darkness. I had ideas as to what was going to happen. They had our passports, all the information possible from us, and our bikes. Because we were going this direction, I knew for certain that they weren't through with us yet. My thoughts were of locks and seclusion.

Ahead I could see light coming through cracks around an ill–fitting door. As we approached, a soldier opened it for us to enter.

Stepping inside we entered into either a small theater or briefing room. To the left was a low stage with a desk in the middle and a banister around it. Ahead and to the right were rows of wooden benches where we took advantage and sat down for the first time in at least four hours.

Sitting at the desk was a non–uniformed man in his mid–forties. He must have been roused from his bed since he wasn't groomed. His hair and beard weren't combed, and he was leaning forward holding our passports, pointing at us one at a time, laughing.

He was laughing so hard that I mistook him for being a sadistic butcher, thinking to myself that the end of the trail is near. Sherm Cooper spoke up in our defense, "We came in peace. We were only passing through your country." The non-uniformed man never stopped his pointing and chuckling to himself.

How wrong a first impression can be. If only we could have looked over his shoulder, except for Bettencourt, we would have been laughing too, seeing gentlemen's pictures in the passports and trying to figure out which bearded, dusty, unwashed, tired example of the Caucasian race fit the description and image he was holding.

No doubt, for years this fellow, who was probably the base commander, has told the story about the six white dustballs who came riding motorcycles out of the Serengeti and stumbling into his army camp.

One more round of questioning, this time no guns and more like a get–acquainted session, or it could have been another form of cross–examination. Whatever the reason for moving us to this second building, the fear of being riddled by bullets for an unexpected move or the dropping of a hat was over.

He still had a big grin on his face when he told us we could leave. Standing tall and looking us over from head to foot, he shook his head, never before seeing that much dust on the move.

Because we were leaving, he could return to the soft companionship of his lady. As for us, we were totally ignored walking back to our bikes, starting the engines and again leaving only our tracks but taking unforgettable memories.

It was a lonesome ride back through the dimly lit streets of Musoma. The darkness couldn't conceal the recent past, when cars and trucks used these streets, industry gave families a purpose, and a staffed hospital could have given aid and comfort to our injured friend.

A nation where politicians lack compassion and the resolution for compromise is a nation where its people revert back to self–preservation.

So it was that night that we camped on the knoll of the second hill south of the city at a quarter 'til three. Our host this past evening didn't serve, so we were hungry until morning.

The next day was spent at a grass airstrip and a small office. That morning Bill Record was able to locate a plane to come in and fly Dick out to Nairobi, Kenya, to get his broken shoulder set. During this time an official looking Tanzanian walked through where we were just sitting around and informed us we had to be out of their country by midnight. We wouldn't leave Bettencourt to fend for himself, so we stayed with him until the plane arrived and left, taking him to Nairobi.

By 4:30 p.m. Dick was airborne in a twin engine Beachcraft piloted by a good–looking fellow with flowing brown hair, wearing a leather bomber jacket and a light tan silk scarf. Dick deserved to be in good hands after the punishment he endured the past twenty-six hours without vocal complaint.

Dick Bettencourt passed away from natural causes December 1991, at his home with his family and close friend, Dick Ambrosia. As a result of his meeting with the Pucker Bush, Dick walked with a slight bend at his shoulders. Until a very few weeks before his passing, he was still a highly skilled, hard charging dirt rider. During his last day, he sat on the side of his bed and on his VCR watched himself and friends riding the Colorado 500. God Speed, dear friend.

We had no desire to find out how much credence to give the demand to be out of their country by midnight. It was a ride of a few long hours of hard traveling on bumpy gravel roads with one river to cross. Rather than a river, it may have been backwater from Lake Victoria, as there didn't seem to be any current. Arriving at the river, we found a low, flat barge with a small gasoline engine with reduction gears and a pulley wheel. Unanchored to each bank were pulleys with a cable running through all and around the engine pulley. All that could be taken across at one time was a small load using the engine. This took a lot of precious time, of which we had little to spare.

Sherm and I were the last to cross as daytime was turning into evening. Then darkness set in with no rest for us. We just kept riding. Between ten and eleven o'clock, Sherm clutched in and stopped. He told me he had to rest for awhile. I said, "We can't stop here," pointing over my left shoulder. "That's either a fort or a prison." Because we were so near the frontier, it must have been the towers of a fort we could see above the trees in the darkness.

This was a two–track, high-crown, fine-grit, gravel road not at all easy to travel. Sherm didn't make it two miles before he crashed and crashed hard. He highsided just in front of me with a heavy body–slam. The bike, having no conscience, pounded onto him. He sure didn't need this. His neck was still in his own home–made neck brace. In a few minutes he was walking, talking, and hurting but not necessarily in that order.

Arriving at the first barrier to crossing the frontier into Kenya, we caught up with our other riders. Our headlights had been watched for miles from this high location. They told us no one was around, but with our headlights being the last ones, about twenty armed soldiers came out of the bush from both sides, opening the gate for us to pass. No doubt they knew we were coming.

The immigration building a few miles ahead was similar to a truck stop where truck cargoes years ago could be examined under a roof. We parked under this roof and were directed inside to meet with an immigration officer who, I'm certain, was also expecting us. It was midnight!

His office was cement gray, plain, with nothing to give it life. It had two doors and one window with blinds closed toward the traffic side. This room had a bright overhead light. On the walls were two pictures. One I did not know, but the other was readily recognizable as Jomo Kenyatta, Kenya's George Washington and current president.

There were chairs for everyone. As we walked in, a man behind the desk requested that we be seated. He was the immigration officer, wearing civilian clothes, young, about five-feet ten inches tall, slim and reeking with authority. He stood on his left foot, putting his right foot on the backedge of the desktop, leaning forward to get his face closer to ours while resting his right elbow on his protruding knee. He told us up front the rules for leaving their country and the penalties for getting caught smuggling money out. We would be held and face the punishment for the crime. Then he explained how he would catch us. Either he was guessing or he speculated that we had cashed hard currency and the demand for us to leave the country in such a hurry provided no opportunity to use it. This man may have been young, but he had been around the horn a couple of times. I was twice his age and didn't possess the ability to smuggle a smile out of a funny farm.

The next thing he said was, "If I conduct a search and find money hidden in your socks ...." In my socks! How did he know that? That's where I always hide my money. He kept up this jargon, but by now I wasn't listening. I just reached down into my right sock, pulled my hard–earned cash out and placed it on the desktop. The summit of my adventure had been reached. As for the remainder of that night, from then until morning it was all downhill.

199

Sherm was very beat up and hurting, but by morning light he was born again, and we awoke hearing his sunrise song, "Out of those sheets; onto your feet. Let's get these bikes rolling."

XXXIX

INTO THE LAND OF THE MASAI
2 Degrees South – 37 Degrees East

During my first afternoon in one of Nairobi's city parks, I met another adventurer from America who spent a few hours telling me of his near fatal experience west of Arlet in the Sahara Desert. He also related a face to face meeting with a gorilla while he was crawling through a low trail in the jungles of Equatorial Africa.

Like myself, he had become slim from dehydration and traveling long hours. He then pulled off his shirt and showed me some of the results of a severe beating he endured during a robbery just a few nights previous right there in that very park. Even with this story still fresh, I endured a similar beating and robbery about a week later for the same reason, walking alone in a place I shouldn't have been.

Not wanting to spend an uneventful evening in camp, I had ridden my bike uptown and left it in a hotel private drive, then walked to a theater just a few blocks to the west.

During that early tropical evening in this beautiful old British city of Nairobi, I stopped to read the posters under the light of a theater's marquee. It depends on what Mother Earth is compared to when we say it's a small world. Well, a small world it was. Jerome Zuravsky, who had left us back in Zaire and caught an airplane to this city, walked up and startled me by slapping me on the shoulder and greeting me with, "Hello, Jerry." The initial conversation was cut short when he proposed that I take his place to meet a Masai at his hotel room.

At first thought, it seemed evident he was ducking out of view for a few hours by going into the theater. In other words, he was squirming out of an appointment that was to take place at eight o'clock that evening. His request was for me to take his place in meeting a Masai who would assist in buying African artifacts.

Zuravsky was apparently afraid that it was a setup for a robbery. I wasn't the least bit apprehensive of meeting the Masai. On the contrary, I was extremely anxious for the experience of meeting someone so culturally different from myself, so I took the door key and left for his room in one of Nairobi's better hotels.

Arriving early gave me a chance to take a real shower where I controlled the water's temperature, soaped and soaked. What a treat that was. I still had time after dressing to turn his TV on, a first since November back in Iowa.

At eight o'clock on the button there was the expected knock on Zuravsky's hotel room door. Would it be a spear wielding Masai rushing in to rob and plunder or a Masai posing at the threshold waiting for an invitation to enter, hoping to be a legitimate intermediary for the purchase of African Artifacts? It didn't take long for me to find out. I got up, switched off the tube and opened the door.

Standing there was a rather clean-cut Masai wearing a dark short-sleeved shirt, slacks and oxford shoes. However, he was extremely irritated because of my commonplace appearance rather than the big spender from Phoenix.

In the next half hour of conversation, the subject changed from the implications of his being stood up to making arrangements for him to take me into the Great Riff Valley to spend time with the feared Masai tribesmen. During conversation he explained that he was a son of a chief and the next to youngest son of his father's tenth of twelve wives. We both agreed to rendezvous at a car rental agency early the following morning.

By first light Jim Squires, Ralph Hurtienne and I had our tents down and rolled. We ate a good breakfast of oatmeal, bread and coffee and left on the first leg of a day with a people unique from all others.

The Masai loosely claim lands in the Great Riff Valley including lands in all directions as far as the eye can see from the peaks of Kilimanjaro.

When one enters the land of the Masai, he is on his own. It is well know that this is their land and no government forces will enter for a rescue if misadventure occurs.

The Masai has maintained a spear-wielding army for many centuries. And it is told, mostly true I'm sure, that there has never been a Masai taken by slave traders, no Mau Mau ever plundered in their land and that the lions are so fearful of their warriors these ferocious felines only prowl at night.

At the rental franchise early the following morning, the operator wouldn't even consider leasing to the Masai but didn't hesitate for a moment giving me the keys to one of his rental cars.

The month before, I was inside a vehicle for a short period of time. That was the taxi ride in Bangui with Barney Koski running along side. This was the second time traveling inside a vehicle rather than on a saddle in nearly three months.

Take it from me, sitting inside an automobile looking out a window frame is just about as exciting as watching pillows fight. One has no direct contact with Mother Earth or its environment. However, the car worked fine as the four of us could visit and learn as we traveled together.

Just a few miles into the famous valley after leaving the city, we headed west on a sandy track. We had to decelerate, nearly stopping, to avoid being overrun by giraffes.

Seeing giraffes on the move, one stops to think. Were they put together by the city planning committee? The hind legs don't seem to be in sync with the front legs. It's as if one set of legs doesn't know what the other set is doing.

The hyenas that we saw, on the other hand, are from that other sub culture. We saw them just hanging around. They were recognizable by their slouched posture, foul language and their arm and body markings. They would get their night's nourishment where the alley converges with the street. Hyenas are not only scavengers, eating what is left by others, but are also predators, giving rise to the uneasiness one knows when walking alone feeling the need for night security.

In this Great Riff Valley of East Africa, there is a high differential of women over men. I have been told the reason for this is that Masai women bear more daughters than sons.

If the gender of Germany's Third Reiche could have been controlled, had they discovered the secret of gender selection, they would have produced young men for their armies in such great numbers that their frozen starved bodies would still be decomposing on the Russian Eastern Front.

The women in waiting all over the world say and believe the same, "He'll be back. He promised." But for the Masai girl, he never returns. It isn't her seducing contemporary in another village, but rather, it is the voluptuous almond-eyed blond in her fur wrap: the most treacherous female of them all, the lioness. It's not that the lioness stalks the tall handsome warrior of the grasslands. Nor does the warrior entice her with gifts or drinks. Rather, it's that chance meeting where their paths cross, their eyes meet, their hearts throb. His spear is no match for her encompassing embrace.

For centuries, when the sun has risen above the Eastern escarpment, the young Masai will group to stalk and kill a lion to prove his essential attributes for becoming a Masai warrior.

Likewise, in the setting sun, revenge is unknowingly fulfilled. The King of Beasts gluttons on his feast. There is no tough hide or fur to hinder his festive treat, just an old, soiled waistcloth and a broken spear.

> As we gaze beyond our neighbor's fence
> Or travel and perceive, we look,
> But never see what it is for them to be.
> For, as we're on the move,
> One lives in faith and fantasy.
> It's when we pause to let our roots take
>   hold,
> We must face reality.
> Thus, as I encountered the Pygmy,
> The Masai or the natives
> In the plush jungle's tranquility,
> I would like to stay and roam with them.
> But, alas, I always return to my own
>   security,
> My loving family.

Driving in a south and southwest direction, we skimmed along on their smooth trail. After an hour of driving, we saw the only permanent building anywhere in this broad valley. It was brown of color, about the size of an old one-room country school house and not unlike, on the outside, the appearance of an old Western trading post.

We came to a stop near the west end of the building. After the other three of us pitched in some Kenyan money, our new Masai acquaintance went inside the trading post to purchase a bolt of cloth, the best gift a Masai chief could receive.

Leaving the hot car's interior, I went over to the shade and leaned against one of the poles that was supporting the canopy on the front entrance of the building.

Three Masai warriors came running up from out of the grassland to this trading post. If this had been a Hollywood gay bar, these fellows would have been the life of the party.

Of course, all they had on were their little waist garments that drape over the right shoulder and tie at the left side. These warriors were six feet tall, erect, wiry and carrying spears with long blades.

Two of them went inside. The third stopped without an utterance or any noticeable body language. We looked at each other to see who was the strangest.

I may be a bit strange, admitting to crashing through firecracker laced, exploding walls of fire, or crossing the Reo Negro River in Guatemala on a rail-less twenty inch wide, two-hundred-foot-long, high bridge while riding double on a BMW. If these things are strange, it's simply a matter of concentration that doesn't outwardly show.

On the other hand, the Masai warrior shows all, including the fact that he is not wearing underwear. The tribal marking was a two-inch wide row of welts from just left of the navel, stretching a path over his left shoulder and beginning down the back. The face, too, showed more tribal and father's identification. On each cheekbone, and downward, were three very prominent scars forming the shape of the three toes of a crow's foot. The crown of his head was adorned with double rows of beads converging at the mid-forehead with larger beads swinging loosely at the upper bridge of the nose. His hair was colored with ocher and held in place using mutton fat.

Saving the most to the last, I observed his ears. No doubt, this warrior and I both took a second look at each other's ears. Now my ears are probably similar to your ears. That's what makes them so unusual to the Masai

Now, I have seen a multitude of fantastic ears. Some have been stretched, some punctured with wooden pins, some with bones. I've seen a pair of ears with the ivory tusk of the wild boar protruding. It's common to see ears that looked like elongated black pretzels, but these three had pretzeled ears that not only dangled, but hung down over their shoulders.

We looked at each other's expressionless faces, both apparently in wonder, then broke eye contact when he entered the general store as our city Masai came out carrying a bolt of printed cloth.

Leaving the trading post in the hot morning sun, we traveled mostly south on a winding, dust-covered road. There was tall grass on all sides, and the escarpments of the valley were beyond our sight.

At the first village we stopped over a hundred yards away. Our Masai ran into the village, then soon returned informing us that the chief was in his other village. At that village we were able to pull up closer before we parked.

This was a typical Masai village, at least in lion country. The village was circular, formed from round, hard, walled huts adjoining each other to form a formidable wall to the outside. The single entrance was just wide enough for cows to pass through.

Outside the entrance lay a thorny tree that had been cut and brought to the entrance and used at night as an unpenetratable gate. To close the gate, the tree was merely pulled in by the trunk, leaving the thorny limbs to the exterior.

Inside, the courtyard was grassless with three large mounds of cow dung in different states of dryness. Cow dung, along with sticks, was used as the Masai's building material. Each morning after the cows were driven outside to graze, the fresh dung was swept up and placed on the freshest pile.

The adult inhabitants were all women, other than their husband chief. The children were very young. When the boys and girls reach puberty, they both are circumcised after which they leave their village to live with another relative. If they don't die of infection from this mutilation, their adult life begins.

In my vague understanding of Masai culture, some of the young men endure long and anguishing preparations to become Morans, the Warriors. Others become herdsmen. The girls that do not become one of the chief's wives follow the youthful men and live near their camps.

The chief's cattle are brought within the village each night. Where or how his herdsmen sleep, I wasn't told, but I would guess they slept outside with the lions.

Each of the chief's sons, upon reaching adulthood, receives five cows to start his herd. However, if one of the boys is caught having sexual intercourse before circumcision, that boy will have one or more of his future herd taken from him. I do not know the penalty, if any, for the girl.

As we were getting acquainted, the chief presented the appearance of being a hard-boiled egg. His twenty or thirty wives were of all ages. Each seemed to be a pleasant, caring woman. Because of their good-nautred ways, I personally felt welcome and at ease.

Soon after giving the chief his bolt of cloth, I showed him my camera and indicated that I would like to take pictures. This "Prima Dona" indicated I could only use my camera facing as I was and where my feet were standing. It was made apparent that neither I, nor anyone else, would cross the chief. I put my Pentex up to my eye crosswise, facing forward, fooling the old boy, and got three great shots.

Was I deceitful in getting a beautiful inside picture of his village? I don't think so. We brought a happy change to what my have been a dull day and enough cloth to make wrap-a-arounds for most of his wives. Soon they would be the brightest girls in the valley

The women seemed to be compatible with each other. The mothers who had two or more infants would share with potential mothers who had not yet become pregnant. The children, as small as babies in arms, already had small wood shaves inserted into their ears, starting to change an ear from a collector of sound to a pretzel-shaped head embellishment for the carrying and displaying of attractive ornaments.

208

This "Prima Donna" indicated I could only use my camera facing as I was and where my feet were standing.

I don't know if the old boy liked it or not, but one of his wives invited us into another wife's hut for a meal. Having some idea of their diet and drink, I knew this would be a meal I would forever remember. And it was.

We entered through a small short tunnel, which paralleled the side, then turned inward into the hemispheric interior. The young wife, maybe twenty years of age, already had a cow dung bonfire burning in the center of the floor, giving light enough for us to see the interior. Other than a two-inch hole toward the upper side to let the smoke out, the fire gave the only illumination.

There was nothing cluttering the inside. As with most native people, they had no possessions to create clutter. However, the inside did have dividers using vertical poles creating two bedrooms. The center of each room was left open with parallel horizontal poles making side rails for the two beds. The beds were cowhides pulled taut. Each would sleep one person on a hot night or two on a cool evening. We all sat facing the fire.

The chief sat to my right. Across from me was our city Masai who never stopped talking about the ways of the Masai except when he and the chief had harsh words a few times. It really surprised and concerned me that he talked back to this main man, but he did so with vigor, as if he were on an equal level.

The meal was soon beginning to warm. Our hostess had a gourd with a liquid inside sitting on the floor next to the fire. Above the fire was a sheet of tin, maybe from a rolled out tin can about the size of a sheet of typing paper. The four corners were secured to four small posts.

Our hostess would take a palm full of dough, roll it and pat it until it was thin like a tortilla. She would put it on the tin to cook, meanwhile spreading it with something and turning it over and over. In a few minutes she took the tortilla and tore it into pieces, dropping them into her only bowl. After that she poured warm liquid over the pieces and served with her only spoon. The first person would eat and drink until finished. This process was repeated until it was my turn. After each, she took her cloth and cleaned the bowl and spoon before the next person ate.

By the time it was my turn to eat, thirty minutes had passed. It was beginning to get intensely warm and the smell of the building material was growing potent. By the time I was partially finished, I started to feel faint. Was it the smell of the hot cow dung or the thought of the drink she would hand me after my food?

Seeing the chief watching me or remembering the words of my deceased father, "Gerald, finish your food." Whatever the reason, I got a second wind and finished my bowl full of food. Just as I passed the bowl and spoon back to our cook, she handed me a container with warmed blood mixed with milk and cow urine to drink.

210

Being a guest, I had no choice. However, if I had had a choice, it would have been the same. I had no idea what warm blood tasted like. It was thick, sweet and went down and stayed down. If it had an odor, I wasn't aware of it as the methane was really getting strong.

Since I was the next-to-last to eat and drink, it wasn't too long before I was outside getting some fresh summer air.

During that time a Masai warrior walked into the village. The chief saw him and barked sharply and loudly. The poor warrior stood straight at attention and only replied when the chief was through. His reply was low toned. The chief was pleased with what was said and let him continue as before.

After that, things got quiet so I left the village for a walk beyond the compound. Outside the only activity was a nanny goat giving birth to a little, wet kid. There, attending her, was a Masai woman helping her to bring a new life to their herd.

The Masai didn't seem concerned about my presence. She may have seen me earlier inside the village compound or, as many other women, never gave me a second look. Using body language, I offered to help. She had me hold a leather thong, which was looped around the nanny's neck. She dried the kid, then carried it about fifty feet away and put it down, tying it to a stake with another thong. She then secured the nanny to a stake, keeping them isolated from each other except by sound. It was puzzling as to why this near helpless newborn creature was deprived of the nearness it had been accustomed to only minutes before in the nanny's womb. Instead it was divested of the warmth and rhythmic heartbeating tranquility and made to endure brightness and vast expanses of Mother Nature.

Seeing the still wet kid emitting the odor of birth, tied near the tall grass, was a reminder of live minnows on a trout line. Who knows what predators linger in the grass.

Evening would soon be approaching in the light tan grasslands of this, the wide deep Riff Valley. During each evening the cows were brought into the village area. The fresh ones were milked and, according to rotation, the cows whose turns are up would be bled.

We were told that a bull, nearly full grown, would be killed in a nearby village, and its meat divided with the village we were visiting. The killing would be done by three Masai holding the animal, one on each ear and one on the tail. Apparently the leverage is such that a fourth Masai can put his fingers, pressing downward, over the two nostrils. The other hand presses upward on the lips of the mouth, holding tight for many, many minutes until the bull dies of suffocation.

The Masai women lived as in another world. Their attitude was pleasant and to each other, compatible and friendly. Their counterparts were another story altogether. The men retain a stern, repugnant temperament.

This stern, no-nonsense inclination is an attribute in retaining their little corner of Africa. As unusual as their society is, it must work. For through the years the threshing machine of time has shaken out the undesirable seeds from their land. The sovereign roots of the Masai people still cling to the valley and the plateaus in sight of Mt. Kilimanjaro.

The influence of the early Arabs who trekked south is heard in their language, in the more narrow faces and the lighter colored skin. They are much different from the Kikuya neighbors. Let's hope they each retain their colorful culture for more centuries than what have passed.

XL

NEVER RUN FROM A MAD ELEPHANT
3 Degrees South – 39 Degrees East

The sun was setting in a reddish glow over the western foothills as I was motoring past Kenya's Tsavo National Park on the road from Nairobi to Mombasa and the Indian Ocean.

I was looking to my left as the road meandered through the low sandhills in a southeasterly direction. The soil and the thorn trees were red. Everything had a reddish hue illuminated by the evening's setting sun. Among the scattered thorn trees and brush were a few boulders roughly the size of overturned bathtubs. My attention was drawn to a massive boulder standing out of place approximately a hundred yards from the road. There was something wrong with its shape and the way it was standing. I slowed down and stopped to further scrutinize this abnormality.

The enormous monstrosity wasn't a rock, but the largest elephant I had ever seen. Using binoculars I could see he was facing toward me with the evening sun in his eyes.

I stayed on my bike watching this immobile creature for a few minutes. He must have been twelve feet high and nearly half as wide as he was tall. That is when I began to realize what a tremendous picture he would make. He was standing in soil the color of some of Georgia's sandy-red clay or that of the Texas Arkansas Red River Valley. Just imagine this: getting a photo of the world's largest land animal in such a unique setting.

Everything was cast in a reddish tint. It was like all the rocks had rusted, leaving their red dust to blend into the surroundings, and at that hour they were highlighted by the evening rays of the sun, tinted with a rosy glow from the moisture laden atmosphere.

213

This leather-gray descendent of the mammoth just stood there in a blush of dust, exercising his sovereign authority. The last thing I wanted to do was disturb him, but at that moment my greatest desire was to capture his magnificent stature on film.

Pondering my chances of walking up to him with my camera in hand it seemed to be a logical gamble. The setting sun was shining directly in his eyes. There was no way in the world he could see me in this stone-quiet, late afternoon. Furthermore, if I approached him with the sun to my back, slowly and in complete silence, I would be in a position to get a shot to enjoy for a lifetime.

I was in a position to take an unusual photograph of an elephant in an entirely reddish coloration, unprotected and in the wild.

To begin this photography session, I hid behind my bike to place a 3X converter behind my 55mm lens, giving me 165mm lens so I could stay back far enough not to offend him, just in case my breath was offensive.

People who stop and take pictures are always by themselves. No one wants to be a buddy with a camera nut who spends half an hour crawling, climbing or just fiddling around trying to achieve what he thinks will be a once in a lifetime shot.

So it was on the road to Mombasa. I took off my helmet and jacket, along with my extra camera equipment, and placed it all behind my bike.

With my Pentex hanging around my neck, the lens pointing downward to prevent the glass from reflecting and alerting my coveted subject, I advanced slowly and quietly through the soft sandy loam, keeping my breathing as muffled as possible. Getting closer, I brought the camera up to see if I was close enough to frame in the big boy. He wasn't close enough on the first attempt, so I walked ten or twelve steps closer. I brought the camera up to try again. This time he nearly filled the lens, framed in a rose tinted background. I may have had adrenaline pumping, but with the kind of rush you get in the excitement of nearly completing an outstanding achievement.

Who could have believed an iceberg would float so far south as to intersect with the *Titanic*? Or the century's worst English Channel storm would hit the Normandy coast on D day? Or that I would have forgotten to cock my camera?

Eyeball to eyeball a mere hundred feet away was a peaceable giant; but when I pressed my thumb on the chrome lever and cocked my Pentex, lightning struck, Mt Vesuvius erupted and that elephant went completely crazy.

Never in my life have I known of an animal having a temper tantrum. This beast of many tons was out of control. First, his ears opened up into the largest heart I've ever seen, nearly as wide as he was tall. His trunk came up with his ears going back and forth. Then he came forward and grabbed a thorn tree near its base using his tremendous trunk. He pulled the tree, roots and all, straight up out of the ground, held it high above his head, then started slamming it down back and forth. He raised the tree above his head again and again hitting down with all of his might while moving from side to side. The huge elephant appeared to have gone completely insane, beating the tree so violently and so many times, it was reduced to the size of a fence post.

That elephant, most emphatically, did not want to be photographed.

My memory flashed back a few years to the weekly television program of *Wild Kingdom*. I remembered they advised against running from elephants. For, if I moved or caused a sound, he would have trampled me so far into the East African sand, my body would be nothing but nutrients for deep-rooted vegetation. Rather than me, it was the innocent thorn tree having its life terminated and devastated to an unrecognizable scattering of splinters.

Slowly I started moving only my legs, taking small quiet steps backward, never moving an eyeball or my upper body in any way. I may have stopped breathing as I tiptoed backwards. I knew if I did as little as break a twig, take a breath or make a noise in the sand while he had his ears up, those sound detectors would zero in on me like a smart bomb hitting Baghdad.

When my heels came to an incline, I knew I had missed any bushes that may have been near my retreat. The incline was the road. I backed up, still maintaining my discipline until I felt the bike.

Backing into my bike was not like being home, but at least I had reached the security of having something between us. From behind my enduro I watched the elephant. Minutes passed, but his violent aggressive behavior did not diminish. He kept thrashing the tree trunk with all of his force, raising it above his head, repeatedly bashing it to the ground from side to side.

To quote Admiral Yomamato after the ill-advised attack on Pearl Harbor, "All that was accomplished was to arouse a sleeping giant."

While standing on my knees behind the bike, I put my unused camera away, then donned both my jacket and helmet. I mounted my bike; and, with its usual one kick, I was on my way.

Donald Kaull once asked in his newspaper column, "Wouldn't it be nice to just get on your motorcycle and ride off into the sunset?"

To give a belated answer, "Yes it is. It's a fabulous experience to climb on your motorcycle and ride off into the sunset."

XLI

SCRIMMAGE ABOVE THE CORAL REEF
5 Degrees South - 39 Degrees East

In my youth, dad cautioned me pertaining to the perils of exploring by myself. I always remembered these words of wisdom, but rarely, if ever, did I heed them.

This day, as many, I should have adhered to the advice of my dear dad. For, as has occurred in more situations that I can recall, I again escaped by the skin of my teeth. However, with all of my shortcomings, I do have a positive attribute. That is the lightening fast flashbacks, giving me instant reactions in bad situations.

We had set up camp in an area above the beach located south of Mombasa, Kenya, on the Indian Ocean. After breakfast I took care of some chores, then left on foot in a northern direction along the beach, subsequently climbing a cliff overlooking the coral reefs. There was an enclave below the cliff. From the cliff I could see movement of the strange and unusual sea life below. For a better view, I descended and sat down on an exposed, eroded stone, watching with a curious wonderment, life below the surface.

On returning to the cliff overlooking the sea, I found three young thugs waiting to rob me. The first approached from the front and said, "Jamo." His eyes flashed past my left shoulder. A moment later the remaining two grabbed me from behind.

Instantly I remembered wrestling coach Brand, screaming, "turn into your opponent before he can secure his hold." Then turning to break the near hold and spinning my body, I broke loose.

In the melee I lost my glasses, ruined my trunks and sustained deep bruises on my rib cage, both hips and upper arms.

There is no way that I can say it was worth it. If I had been robbed and thrown off the cliff onto the razor sharp coral, it would have been nearly fatal. However, for the experience of gazing at long whitish legs coming out of seashells, once was enough.

At rest in Manyara

XLII

MY LAST HURRAH
4 Degrees South – 36 Degrees East

In the American way, arriving at Manyara National Park, we merely turned left entering their predator's picnic grounds, unaware of any restrictions. The lane into the park was of loose sand, winding past the larger trees, descending for about a mile until it reached the park's small office complex.

We parked our motorcycles in front of the complex and within thirty minutes a park ranger had us loaded into his Land Rover.

Then from the seats, or standing and looking out of the pop-top of the Land Rover, we thrilled at seeing from close range the life and behavior of some of Africa's animals in the wild.

Manyara, as are most wild game parks, is unique, and yet similar in some aspects to other parks. The wild animals of Manyara, like those of Ngorongora Crater, are not entrapped. However, virtually all of the non-flying creatures in both parks live as if they were entrapped.

A few animals may enter or leave Ngorongora by descending or climbing its two-thousand-foot crater wall. In Manyara an animal would have three choices to get out. It could climb the western escarpment, swim salty Lake Manyara or penetrate through the jungle.

Because of this near entrapment in Manyara's crowded animal community, the lion, as an example of this novel environment, has adapted to sleeping in trees. They find a large tree with horizontal limbs and peaceably sleep their idle time away. The big cats merely straddle the thickest limb they can find, resting their long bodies and heads, letting all four legs and tail drape downward.

On returning to the office building, all was not well. An army truck with a few soldiers was waiting to take us into custody.

"Climb up in the truck. The Colonel want's to see you," was the afternoon greeting by one of Tanganyika's finest.

Dressed in military tans, with a leather-holstered persuader strapped firmly on his right hip, his one liner moved us from conversation to stunned silence. We reached for the high tailgate on this military four-by-four.

Using the heavy-duty trailer hitch as a step and the tailgate as a handhold, we did as the soldier in authority commanded. We climbed up and into the truck.

While the whine of gears remained in low, we drove back up the sandy lane to a gravel road. From there we had to hang on to the stock racks and breath slowly as dust was rolling in from the back and both sides.

No more than thirty minutes passed until we drove into a stockade. I wasn't able to see much as we swung around with the back of the truck toward a long warehouse type building with a high dock.

We were ordered to climb down and line up facing the dock. Already standing in a crisp military stance were five men, all in dark-brown uniforms, two men on each side of the colonel.

There was no doubt who was in charge, for facing us in a well–pressed uniform, a military hat, standing spread eagle, his hands clasped behind his back, stood "George C. Scott" in Hollywood's portrayal of General Patton.

It was no laughing matter. He demanded respect, and we were respectful. We, too, stood with our hands behind our backs, completely attentive.

The officer's first utterance was to inform us we had entered the wild game park of Manyara in open vehicles, which was very dangerous and an infraction of the law. He continued by informing us our penalty was to return to the park and push our motorcycles by hand out of the park.

That punishment may not seem difficult or harsh, but the thought of pushing my motorcycle through soft sand over what appeared to be an uphill narrow road was going to be a long tiring way to spend an evening.

Bill Record, using logic, stepped forward acknowledging our error in judgment, apologized for riding into their park in an open vehicle. He also stated the danger of being on foot and pushing our motorcycles during the lateness of the day when big animals are on the prowl.

The colonel unclasped his hands from behind his back, leaned forward and nodded his head. He just stood there for a moment, then gave, with a hand gesture, one of the natives a command in Swahili.

With this, the ordeal was over. Only the dusty, bumping ride back to our bikes remained.

Riding slowly after retrieving the Hondas, I looked down at the soft sand, thankful the power to leave was from internal combustion engines, rather than tired, sore legs.

I have escaped punishment by reprieve, by trickery and by elusion. Reprieve doesn't make for a good story, but is a thousand fold easier on the nerves.

Leaving the wild game reserve, we turned to the right, through a small town of Mto Wa Mbu, continuing east and south for two hours. This uneventful evening motorcycle ride allowed me time to reminisce on the day in Manyara, picturing the beast of the jungle, the gentle, the huge and the ferocious. I also recalled the environment where they lived, wrapped in vines. There were the gigantic termite mounds, each a home for millions of flying fiber eaters. There were also the massive trees, which are a haven for many creatures that fly or climb. Still a few retain the spirits of their native ancestral souls.

The sun was to our backs as darkness was setting in when we slowed, then came to a stop on the crest of a high plateau overlooking the Great Riff Valley. From that vantage point we located what appeared to be an ideal camping place.

After descending the dirt road, possibly a quarter of a mile, we turned right for a few hundred yards and stopped. Except for one thing, this was a perfect location to spend the night. It was a level, smooth enclave extending into the valley's gentle wall. There were boulders on all sides except the front, which featured the path.

The exception was that this was Masai country. Our rider from Montana expressed his opinion loudly to Bill Record, pleading to turn back a few miles where there would be less danger from the Masai warriors. His pleas were well founded but futile, as our tents were being set up as he spoke.

With the moon of the Southern Hemisphere rising above the eastern horizon and the dew of the night clinging to the green, angular, vinyl sides of the tent, our camp must have been glowing for miles across the valley floor.

By the time Jack Hawthorne had our meal ready and we sat around eating, the moon was shining from an ever-higher angle. It may have been romantic for the Masai in the valley below. However, we were uneasy being in the limelight of our earth's celestial body.

During the night, lightly sleeping, I became totally awakened by a five-word, singing chant. Over and over this verse was repeated. I got up, and looked out from the netted window of the triangle–shaped tent. All I saw was the valley swathed in moonlight. Staying at the netted window, I memorized the flowing syllables coming from far below. At last they were inaudible as the line of sight was disrupted by high rocks and brush.

Again, I lay back to rest and sleep, but awoke hearing the melodic five-word chant louder and much closer. I wormed out of my sheet–lined sleeping bag, wearing my jockey shorts. This time knowing there was a group of Masai near, I put on my sneakers, pulling the laces tight, thinking I could run faster with tightly laced shoes.

I crouched down, turning around in the darkness of my tent. I found the zipper tab and pulled up, opening the end flaps, then crawled out and around my tent on hands and knees, going far enough forward to obtain a view up the path. Just as I looked up the path toward the dirt road on which we had traveled, I saw two rows of long spear blades flashing in the bright moonlight.

They were moving fast and being held high. At first I thought the warriors were leaving the valley and everything was fine in my world. It was when they intersected the path we were on that they turned toward us at their perpetual fast pace. Now, that caused me extreme trauma. I didn't run. I couldn't yell to warn the others. I just stayed frozen with my hands at the edge of the path. I moved nothing but my eyes, watching, hoping their hours of chanting and running had them in a blind trance. What bothered me, chanting or not, they knew where to turn. They also had to have seen the reflection of our dew-laden tents from far below on the valley floor and during their run up the dirt road of the escarpment.

I didn't have a clue as to what they were doing. In the bright moonlight, lions do not prowl. This gave the warriors security, so the only reason I could imagine for their running toward our camp from the valley below was because we were there.

For two or three minutes they were out of my sight because of the angle of the path. Then, above the boulders, the moonlight reflected on their oncoming long blades, four, and then, four more. Between the blades were the Masai's embellished, beaded foreheads, all bouncing to the rhythmic five word chant. By the time I could see their shining brown shoulders with arms bent tight at the elbows, I knew I would soon be meeting my Maker and my body giver. It appeared I would be giving up this body to the step-country's scavengers, with only my bones, and hopefully my soul to survive. I resented dying like a coward on my hands and knees.

My best chance was to not move. My skin was light dusty tan over the sandy soil. The only things that might reflect were my dingy white jockey shorts. To move would reveal my location if they hadn't already seen me.

A warrior, seeing an unexpected movement could, by reflex, jab his spear forcefully for his self-preservation.

In the last minute, as the warriors approached, I held my breath, making my body completely devoid of movement. Around the corner boulder they came, through the outer edge of our camp. Their bodies were tall and lean; they were still rhythmically chanting, holding those long spears at the ready. They charged past, nearly stepping on my hands.

It was over. The Masai warriors were gone.

I tried to get up, but by body felt like a huge cotton balloon. My nerves' motor impulses must have run wild. Without seeing or feeling my skin, I would have sworn my body was of enormous size. I didn't feel normal again until I rubbed my hands over my arms, body and legs.

However, it was those men who amazed me. Realizing the fast, unbroken stride of eight superbly conditioned men who, no doubt, were just going somewhere awed me. They had run up the three thousand foot southwest escarpment, then paralleled the upper rim in two disciplined rows while holding with their right arm and hand, the long blade spears. I may have been in a nervous state, but if they were panting, it wasn't audible.

By morning the sun again rose above the Great Riff Valley's far escarpment, and I crawled from my tent for the last time. To again repeat an old proverb, "Once you have drunk the waters of Africa, you will forever thirst to return."

AFRICAN TREKKERS
SCHEDULED FOR FULL AFRICAN CROSSING
87 DAYS, 8756 MILES

JERRY SMITH
HEDRICK, IA

SHERMAN COOPER
TRENTON, NJ

DON MURK
MINNEAPOLIS, MN

BARNEY COSKI
TACOMA, WA

BILL RECORD
MANCHESTER, NY
(PLANNED AND ORGANIZED THE AFRICAN TREK)

SCHEDULED FOR FIRST HALF
CEUTA TO BANGUI, CENTRAL AFRICAN REPUBLIC

DAVID RAY
LORAIN, OH

ROGER NOBEL
HANOVER, MA

CARL BRECHT
LAWRENCE, NJ

TIM RICE
DEARBORN, MI

ALEX MALOOF
CAIRO, IL

JOHN PUDDICOMBE
JOLIET, IL

RUSS SWANSON
MINNEAPOLIS, MN

JOHN DESEYN (THE COOK)
TOWN NOT KNOWN

**SCHEDULED FOR SECOND HALF
BANGUI TO FINISH**

DICK D'AMBROSIA
SOUTH WEYMOUTH, NJ

JIM SQUIRES
BLOOMFIELD, MT

DICK BETTENCOURT
WEST BRIDGEWATER, MA

RALPH HURTIENNE
SHEBOYGAN, WI

DEL HAINE
ELMHURST, IL

JEROME ZURAVSKY
TUCSON, AZ

227